Authority and Academic Scribblers

THE INTERNATIONAL CENTER FOR ECONOMIC GROWTH is a non-profit research institute founded in 1985 to stimulate international discussions on economic policy, economic growth, and human development. The Center sponsors research, publications, and conferences in cooperation with an international network of correspondent institutes, which distribute publications of both the Center and other network members to policy audiences around the world. The Center's research and publications program is organized around five series: Sector Studies; Country Studies; Studies in Human Development and Social Welfare; Occasional Papers; and Reprints.

The Center is affiliated with the Institute for Contemporary Studies, and has headquarters in Panama and a home office in San Francisco, California.

For further information, please contact the International Center for Economic Growth, 243 Kearny Street, San Francisco, California, 94108, USA. Phone (415) 981-5353; Fax (415) 986-4878.

ICEG Board of Overseers

Authority and Academic Scribblers

The Role of Research in East Asian
Policy Reform

Edited by Sylvia Ostry

A copublication of the International Center for Economic Growth,
the National Centre for Development Studies of Australian National University,
and the Economic Development Institute of the World Bank

ICS Press
San Francisco, California

Inquiries, book orders, and catalog requests should be addressed to ICS Press, 243 Kearny Street, San Francisco California 94108. Telephone: (415) 981-5353; FAX: (415) 986-4878. To order call tollfree **(800) 326-0263** in the contiguous United States. Distributed to the trade by National Book Network, Lanham, Maryland.

The cover was designed by Lisa Tranter.

The index was provided by Shirley Kessel.

Library of Congress Cataloging-in-Publication Data

Authority and academic scribblers : the role of research in East Asian policy reform / edited by Sylvia Ostry.

      p.   cm.

Papers developed at a workshop held Dec. 1988 and at a senior policy seminar held in Mar. 1989.

"An International Center for Economic Growth publication."

Includes bibliographical references (p.) and index.

ISBN 1-55815-133-8 (cloth) : $24.95. — ISBN 1-55815-132-X (paper) $12.95

1. East Asia—Economic policy—Case studies—Congresses. 2. Asia, Southeastern—Economic policy—Congresses. 3. Australia—Economic policy—Congresses. 4. New Zealand—Economic policy—Congresses. I. Ostry, Sylvia. II. International Center for Economic Growth.

HC460.5.A58 1991

338.95—dc20

90-26341

CIP

Practical men, who believe themselves to be quite exempt from any intellectual influences, are usually the slaves of some defunct economist. Madmen in authority, who hear voices in the air, are distilling their frenzy from some academic scribbler of a few years back.

—John Maynard Keynes

CONTENTS

TABLES AND FIGURES

PREFACE

Authority and Academic Scribblers presents a glimpse of the nuts and bolts of economic policy making in eight East Asian countries. In examining the role of policy research in formulating economic policy, *Authority and Academic Scribblers* responds to the growing interest in both the relationship between the academic and legislative bodies and the rapid economic growth achieved by some East Asian countries.

This volume sheds light on the types of policies most conducive to growth and the types of governmental and nongovernmental organizations most effective at conceiving and implementing such policies. In many countries the work of policy researchers fails to meet the needs of policy makers, and the authors suggest how to deal with this and other difficulties.

The International Center for Economic Growth is pleased to copublish this book with the National Centre for Development Studies of Australian National University and the Economic Development Institute of the World Bank. Because the dissemination of innovative and useful policy research, as well as the effective communication of policy ideas, is the primary purpose of ICEG, *Authority and Academic Scribblers* is of great importance to the Center. We hope that all who carry out or use policy research will benefit from the analysis in this volume.

Nicolás Ardito-Barletta
General Director
International Center for Economic Growth

March 1991
Panama City, Panama

ACKNOWLEDGMENTS

These papers were initially developed at a workshop in December 1988 by a small group of scholars working on the economics of liberalization in their own countries. A Senior Policy Seminar, moderated by Sylvia Ostry, followed in March 1989, with politicians and government representatives from East Asian countries participating in a lively discussion.

The Economic Development Institute of the World Bank, in particular Sid Chernick, Vinyu Vichit-Vadakau and Hyung Ki Kim, planned the workshop and seminar.

The National Centre for Development Studies hosted both the workshop and the seminar in Canberra. Brian Brogan was the project manager, Maureen Liu the administrator. Margaret Callan edited the original drafts. Centre staff, notably Maree Tait, May Stinear, and Rae Fry, prepared the papers for publication.

I thank all those who contributed to the success of the meeting and the preparation of the book.

Helen Hughes
Executive Director
National Centre for Development Studies

Authority and Academic Scribblers

INTRODUCTION:
RESEARCH AND ECONOMIC LIBERALIZATION

Since the 1960s the rapid economic growth in East Asia has been the focus of a great deal of attention throughout the world. This book responds to the interest in these countries by exploring the contribution of specific economic policies to the countries' dramatic growth and then by investigating the role of research in formulating economic policy.

The enormous success enjoyed by a group of East Asian countries is truly extraordinary, outpacing all developing countries in economic growth and social development. In the 1950s the Republic of Korea and Thailand were among the poorest countries in the world; they are now "middle-income countries." The East Asian industrializing countries and near-industrializing countries are catching up to the industrial countries in productivity and living standards. If all industrializing countries were growing at their pace, development would not be a problem. There would be far fewer poor people in the world, and the great differences between developing and industrial countries would disappear.

This remarkable economic growth is, to a large degree, the result of successful economic policies. Conservative fiscal and monetary policies, which have been more consistently applied in several East Asian countries than in developing countries elsewhere in the world, have resulted in low inflation, stable exchange rates, and microeconomic policies that tended toward outward rather than inward orientation. Compared with economic policy in South Asian and Latin American countries over the past thirty years, economic policies in East Asia have also been less inclined toward public ownership of production outside the natural monopoly, public goods sectors.

The Role of Research in Policy Formulation

In East Asian countries, policies are determined, as they are in all countries, by the interactions of politicians, bureaucrats, and special interest groups of varying degrees of power and competence. This political process has shaped the world's economic successes, as well as its failures, over the past thirty years. Although most of the East Asian countries are not democracies in the European–North American mold, political power does depend on some degree of popular support. And although the policy formulation debate has not been as open as it has been in industrial democracies, it has taken place. (The principal exceptions are China and Vietnam, where technical economic expertise lags far behind most other East Asian countries.)

Research has made a major contribution to the outcomes of policy formulation debates by informing the process within bureaucracies, political arenas, and special interest groups and throughout public debate in the region.

Research reduces the likelihood of ad hoc responses to problems. Using the results of research, decision makers can identify the key economic problems facing a country, formulate a range of policy options, and articulate possible policy responses together with their consequences.

Policy choices and combinations of policies can be improved by

- clearly defining the problems faced

- setting out the principal alternatives available

- clearly identifying the major vested interests likely to be affected by policy changes

- comparing the cost effectiveness of various policies and groups of policies

- ascertaining the trade-offs among policy choices and hence providing a basis for negotiation among vested interests

It is also essential to consider both *structural* issues (such as the allocation of policy oversight to various government departments) and *process* issues (such as cabinet committee and consultative systems).

Successful Policy Research

Some types of research are more useful than others in successful policy formulation. The characteristics of useful economic research are not difficult to define:

- A reasonable database is needed, but data gathering must be cost effective rather than exhaustive; the database must be in the public domain to ensure that it is widely used and hence constantly checked.

- Research needs a sound theoretical base rather than an ideological bent.

- Technical tools must be rigorously used to test alternative policy possibilities.

- An independent institutional base is required for effective research inputs.

- An open debate must ultimately emerge to subject research to domestic and international peer review.

No matter how advanced the theory, how strong the database, or how sophisticated the modeling techniques, the research process also requires good judgment.

During the past thirty years or so most East Asian countries have developed economic policy research capacities that meet such standards. Most have relied heavily on training students abroad (initially at undergraduate and more recently at graduate levels). Returning students staffed universities, bureaucracies, and research organizations. Initially, countries also relied on assistance from research organizations in industrial countries. Harvard University, the University of Wisconsin, the Rockefeller and Ford foundations, and many other universities and research organizations played an important role in building up professional and research skills in East Asian countries.

Although the governments of East Asia devoted considerable resources to economic planning (all of the East Asian countries except Hong Kong had formal five- to seven-year plans for some time at least), planning contributed surprisingly little to building research capacity. Most East Asian countries became dubious about the utility of planning by the 1970s, but paradoxically, they continued to produce plans to satisfy donors. The principal contribution of planning was in the introduction of rigorous cost-benefit methodologies to rank public works projects. Thus, planning de facto combined strategic statements about the direction of growth with public-sector expenditure plans.

The failures of economy-wide planning led to the establishment of a new type of research unit, which focused on policies that lead an economy by price signals to producers and consumers rather than by physical directives. Specialized policy research units, with strong overseas support through staffing and funding, followed the example of the Korea Development Institute (KDI). To retain a well-trained professional and support staff, KDI-type institutes increased low salaries at universities and continued to sponsor both travel abroad by Asian scholars and visits to East Asia by leading overseas economists.

Policy Research and Economic Liberalization: Overview

This volume grew out of a seminar attended by politicians, bureaucrats, and academics from East Asia, Australasia, and international organizations in Canberra, Australia, in March 1989. They discussed their experiences with the liberalization process and the role of policy research in successful development. The background papers and the conclusions of the discussion appeared to be sufficiently novel to merit publication.

The volume begins with chapters on Thailand, Malaysia, and Republic of Korea. Because of their remarkable economic growth, there is perhaps more interest in these three countries than in any of the other five examined in this book. Each of the three, however, has had its own experience with policy research.

Narongchai Akrasanee discusses the role of policy research in Thailand, where well-educated technocrats have been in government posts since the 1960s when economic growth began to accelerate. Macroeconomic policies have been the foundation on which agriculture, industry, and trade could develop. When the research inputs were found to be inadequate for a rapidly growing economy in the 1980s, the Thai Development Research Institute was founded.

Mohamed Ariff discusses the influence of policy research in Malaysia. Malaysia has never had severely distorted economic policies. Consequently it has not required radical policy adjustment. Policy research has not been strong in Malaysia: among the factors responsible have been a lack of interest in research on the part of policy makers and the abstract nature of the research done by academic economists.

Policy reform in the Republic of Korea is discussed by In June Kim. He notes that recently the Presidential Commission on Economic Restructuring established a forum for public debate on economic issues. Commission members came from a broad spectrum of society to investigate a variety of issues. An underlying contribution, however, came from the Korea Development Institute, which established the importance of research for policy reform not only for the Republic of Korea, but for the entire region.

Zhao Dadong discusses the role of policy research in China, which, like the other countries discussed in this book, instituted major economic reforms in the 1980s. Unlike the other countries, however, China had a centrally planned economy. Because the interest in, as well as the practice of, economic research is relatively new in China, there is a shortage of adequately trained researchers and an insufficient database. Chinese policy makers are taking time to understand the importance of an open policy debate for the effective utilization of research in policy making.

Raul V. Fabella discusses the role of research in policy reform in the Philippines, where political, social, and economic circumstances have been quite different than in most East Asian countries. Economic policy began with high levels of protection in the 1950s and then moved to stop-and-go macroeconomic policies. Economic debate was repressed by the government of Ferdinand Marcos and was often distorted by the media. Fortunately Filipino academic economists provided an independent critique of the economic policies of the Marcos government, and they have continued to attempt to influence and stimulate economic reforms under Corazon Aquino's government.

Mari Pangestu points out that in Indonesia the high level of petroleum income was too much of an obstacle to economic reform. The fall in petroleum prices, however, stimulated policy reforms in the 1980s so that the Indonesian economy has performed much better than that of other petroleum-rich countries. Indonesia has been fortunate in having a stable group of policy makers, who were not only concerned with the content of reforms but also with their appropriate sequencing. The importance of public debate has recently been recognized as an important component of policy formulation.

Suiwah Leung illustrates the necessity of support from the private sector in a market economy. In Australia and New Zealand financial liberalization became the starting point for further policy reform. In both countries the economy changed, making liberalization desirable and creating a political climate conducive to change. Ultimately there was little opposition to Australasian financial liberalization because most of the parties involved benefited from it. Public institutions in Australia and New Zealand carried out much of the research necessary for financial liberalization to take place. Nevertheless, there has been strong theoretical support from the academic community, and in the second half of the 1980s a number of think tanks have developed to stimulate the debate, which has also benefited from a strong financial press.

THE ROLE OF POLICY RESEARCH IN THE TRADE AND INDUSTRY REFORMS OF THAILAND

During the past three decades Thailand has had a stable economy and reasonable growth by international standards. The industrial sector, led by manufacturing, has expanded substantially. There has been expansion in manufactured exports since the early 1970s, and significant increases since the mid-1980s. In recent years the country has had substantial foreign-investment inflows and foreign-exchange earnings through tourism and other service incomes.

Before 1960 Thailand had a small manufacturing sector comprised of relatively large-scale government enterprises and mostly small-scale private enterprises. After 1960 incentives for private investment were introduced, and the government concentrated on providing public infrastructure. Economic growth accelerated: the manufacturing sector expanded as a protective tariff regime and investment incentives promoted import-substituting industries. In the 1970s the policy emphasis moved more toward export promotion, and by 1987 manufactured exports were 63 percent of total exports.

After the 1973 petroleum price increases, Thailand's growth rate fell and inflation rose. Nevertheless, with expansionary macroeconomic policies and improving world economic conditions, real growth rates recovered to average 9 percent per year in the period 1975–1978. The second round of petroleum price increases had more serious consequences because Thailand had become more dependent on external trade. Inflation accelerated, the balance-of-payments deficit rose, and the burden of debt servicing increased. Slower industrial growth followed. By 1986, however, an export-led recovery was under way. Domestic prices and interest rates were adjusted downward, investment and tourism were promoted, and domestic economic activity expanded. Foreign investment in Thailand increased rapidly, especially in the export sector.

Until the 1980s Thailand's economic growth was directed through macroeconomic policy. The tariff structure and investment incentives protected the developing industrial sector. Regardless, there were major policy reforms after the second petroleum price increase, when the cost of imports rose dramatically and the government had to borrow heavily abroad. First, the baht was devalued and tied to a basket of currencies rather than the U.S. dollar. Second, the private sector was encouraged by liberalization of business practices. Third, industrial policy emphasized the export sector through promotion activities, tax rebate and refund schemes, and changes to the tariff structure.

As a result, the economic situation has turned around rapidly since 1986. Economic growth has accelerated, export earnings have expanded, and foreign exchange from tourism and investment have helped to alleviate the country's external balance problems. Although some basic economic problems such as rural poverty and disparity in income distribution remain to be solved, it is widely believed that Thailand's overall economic performance will continue to be strong. Some predict that Thailand will join the newly industrializing countries in the 1990s.

The military dominated Thailand's government until recently. Decision making was a closed process, and there was little coordination between government agencies. Since 1980, however, elected politicians have been more important, and the prime minister has appointed a number of technocrats to the cabinet and some academics to be economic advisers. These professionals are open to advice from outside, and there has been much public debate on policy issues. Because Thailand has relied mainly on macroeconomic policy to direct its trade and industry development, policy research has been done overwhelmingly by government agencies. At present there seems to be a demand from policy makers for more independent research. Cooperation between government and independent policy researchers is desirable.

This chapter reviews the industrialization process in Thailand in the last three decades, with an emphasis on trade and industrial policy reforms and the role of policy research in this process. First, there is a historical background of industrial development in Thailand over the past three decades. Second, a description of industrial and trade policy reforms. Third, a discussion of the role of policy research in policy reforms and conclusions about the lessons learned.

Overview of Thailand's Industrial Development in the Post-War Period

Initial conditions for industrial growth. Before World War II Thailand had developed a small manufacturing capacity. The dominant manufacturing industries were rice mills, timber, and other simple processing industries (Ingram 1971). Industrial development policy in the decade following the end of the war was characterized by heavy government involvement in manufacturing: a number of relatively large state enterprises were established. Their products included cement, paper, sugar, tobacco, gunnysacks, and a variety of consumer goods. Private manufacturing activities, on the other hand, were mostly small scale and largely confined to rice mills, sawmills, textiles, and handicrafts. The operation of government enterprises was inefficient due to poor management and widespread corruption, and almost all showed substantial losses.

Around 1960 there was a sharp change in industrialization policy. The government began to reduce its direct involvement in manufacturing and concentrate its efforts on providing public infrastructure, with particular emphasis on electric power, transportation, and communications. It also began active promotion of private investment. In 1959 a Board of Investment was established to administer a new investment promotion law, which provided tax and other incentives to private investors.

Thailand's economic growth accelerated, with the average annual real growth rate of gross domestic product (GDP) rising from about 5 percent in the 1950s to about 8 percent in the 1960s. Average annual real growth of manufacturing was estimated at 6.7 percent between 1952 and 1960 and 10.9 percent between 1960 and 1969. (Economic growth rates in this chapter refer to the average annual growth rate of GDP at constant prices. The national income statistics of Thailand since 1970 have been revised recently by the National Economic and Social Development Board. Growth rates before 1970 cited in this chapter refer to the old GDP series, while those from 1970 onward refer to the revised GDP series. No attempt is made to adjust for consistency between the two series.) The year 1960 is thus frequently seen as the starting point of industrialization in Thailand. At that time the agricultural sector still dominated the Thai economy. It contributed 40 percent of GDP, employed over 80 percent of the country's total labor force, and accounted for nearly 90 percent of the country's total export earnings. Manufacturing, on the other hand, contributed 12 percent of GDP, employed less than 4 percent of the labor force, and accounted for only slightly more than 2 percent of total merchandise exports.

Changes in production and trade structure in the 1960s and 1970s. The expansion of the industrial sector has been rapid since the

TABLE 2.1   Share of Gross Domestic Product by Sector, 1960–1987
(1972 constant prices, percentage)

Sector	1960	1965	1970	1975	1980	1985	1986	1987
Agriculture	40.5	36.3	27.0	24.8	20.6	19.9	19.3	17.6
Mining and quarrying	1.2	1.7	2.9	2.1	2.6	2.5	2.3	2.3
Manufacturing	11.7	14.0	16.0	20.0	21.7	20.7	21.5	22.2
Construction	4.8	5.0	5.3	3.7	4.5	4.2	3.9	3.9
Electricity and water supply	0.3	0.6	1.0	1.6	2.0	2.5	2.7	2.8
Transportation and communication	6.7	6.3	6.5	6.1	6.7	7.2	7.3	7.4
Wholesale and retail trade	15.8	16.5	17.4	17.1	16.9	16.3	16.4	17.1
Banking, insurance, and real estate	1.9	2.6	2.5	2.6	2.8	3.0	2.9	3.0
Ownership of dwellings	2.9	2.4	5.6	5.5	4.8	4.4	4.4	4.3
Public administration and defense	4.6	4.3	4.4	4.7	5.2	5.4	5.3	5.2
Services	9.5	9.7	11.5	11.9	12.2	13.9	13.9	14.2
Gross domestic product	100.0	100.0	100.0	100.0	100.0	100.0	100.0	100.0

NOTE: The national income statistics of Thailand have been revised recently by the National Economic and Social Development Board, and the revised series go back to 1970. Calculation of GDP shares for 1970 and later is calculated from the revised series. GDP shares for 1960 and 1965 are calculated from the old GDP series. No attempt is made to adjust the consistency of the two series.
SOURCE: National Economic and Social Development Board, *National Income Statistics of Thailand*, various issues.

launching of the industrialization program in 1960. The growth of manufacturing exceeded the overall growth of GDP, and the share of manufacturing and other nonagricultural sectors in GDP increased steadily. In the mid-1970s manufacturing, with around 20 percent of GDP, emerged as the second largest sector in the economy, trailing only agriculture (see Table 2.1).

Rapid growth was accompanied by changes in the structure of domestic production and foreign trade. A modern industrial sector developed as a result of increased private investment from both domestic and foreign sources. New industries included textiles, apparel, rubber products, chemical products, and transport equipment. Food, beverages, and tobacco, which dominated the manufacturing sector in earlier years, continued to grow but declined in relative importance (see Table 2.2).

The strategy for industrialization in the 1960s was largely import-substitution oriented. Tariff protection was provided to domestic industries, and the Board of Investment also gave preference to import-competing activities. In the 1970s promotion of manufactured exports began to be emphasized, and the incentive structure was revised to promote exports. Nevertheless, the process of import substitution continues and import-competing industries still receive much protection.

TABLE 2.2   Manufacturing Output by Sector
(1972 constant prices, percentage)

Sector	1960	1965	1970	1975	1980	1985	1986
Food	34.6	25.7	20.6	18.2	14.2	15.1	11.8
Beverages	10.6	10.6	13.0	10.1	9.7	8.9	7.9
Tobacco and snuff	13.0	12.1	10.3	9.5	7.6	5.6	5.7
Textiles	5.2	10.6	9.2	13.9	14.6	15.1	6.1
Apparel	8.0	5.5	4.7	6.3	9.2	11.5	15.1
Wood and cork	4.8	5.2	3.2	2.6	1.4	1.3	1.4
Furniture and fixtures	1.2	1.4	1.3	0.7	0.6	0.7	0.9
Paper and paper products	0.2	0.4	0.7	0.4	1.6	1.5	1.1
Printing and publishing	3.2	2.6	2.2	2.8	2.7	2.4	1.8
Leather and leather products	0.6	0.5	1.0	0.8	0.5	0.7	0.8
Rubber and rubber products	0.6	0.7	1.6	2.2	2.6	1.8	1.3
Chemicals and chemical products	6.8	5.8	6.3	5.4	8.3	8.8	7.6
Petroleum refining and coal	—	4.5	6.1	7.7	5.1	3.9	13.7
Nonmetallic mineral products	2.9	4.0	5.1	5.7	5.6	5.9	6.6
Basic metals	0.4	0.5	1.7	1.1	1.2	0.9	1.1
Metal products	0.4	0.7	1.9	1.5	1.0	1.0	1.9
Repairing of nonelectrical machinery	0.6	1.3	2.3	1.7	1.8	1.9	—
Electrical machinery and supplies	0.6	0.8	1.4	1.5	2.0	1.9	2.1
Transport equipment	5.4	5.9	5.1	6.4	7.9	7.9	7.7
Miscellaneous	0.9	1.1	2.3	1.2	2.2	3.0	4.3
Total	100.0	100.0	100.0	100.0	100.0	100.0	100.0

SOURCE: National Economic and Social Development Board, *National Income Statistics of Thailand*, various issues.

Since 1960 the structure of foreign trade has changed to reflect the structure of production. The share of consumer goods in total imports fell markedly while that of producer goods increased (see Table 2.3). The share of manufactures in total exports increased substantially (see Table 2.4). There has also been significant product diversification of exports. Although Thailand had a wide range of primary products for export (including rice, maize, tapioca, sugar, and a variety of marine products), manufactured products (such as garments, textiles, jewelry, integrated circuits, and canned pineapple) were also important exports by 1980 (see Table 2.5).

As an open economy that relied heavily on imported petroleum and industrial materials, Thailand was affected strongly by the two

TABLE 2.3   Imports by Economic Classification (percentage)

Classification	1961	1966	1971	1976	1981	1986
Consumer goods	39.5	25.9	17.9	13.2	10.7	17.6
Nondurable	32.2	17.7	10.8	7.8	6.3	10.2
Durable	7.3	8.2	7.1	5.4	4.4	7.4
Intermediate products and raw materials	17.9	21.7	29.2	28.3	24.7	28.4
Chiefly for consumer goods	10.9	14.0	18.8	17.5	15.6	18.8
Chiefly for capital goods	7.0	7.7	10.4	10.8	9.1	9.6
Capital goods	25.5	31.3	32.4	27.1	26.4	31.5
Machinery	13.4	18.0	21.7	18.1	17.0	23.0
Others	12.0	13.3	10.7	9.0	9.4	8.5
Vehicles and parts	7.9	10.1	8.2	7.2	4.4	3.7
Fuel and lubricants	10.1	10.3	10.2	23.4	30.1	13.4
Others	(0.7)	0.6	2.1	0.7	3.7	5.4
Total	100.0	100.0	100.0	100.0	100.0	100.0

SOURCE: Bank of Thailand, *Monthly Bulletin*, various issues.

TABLE 2.4   Share of Exports by Sector (percent)

Sector	1961	1966	1971	1976	1981	1986	1987
Agriculture	82.7	76.9	62.2	51.8	47.7	34.3	27.9
Fishing	0.4	1.8	2.0	4.4	4.3	6.4	6.1
Forestry	3.3	2.2	1.5	1.7	0.1	0.3	0.3
Mining	6.6	11.6	13.7	6.7	7.7	2.7	2.0
Manufactur-ing	2.4	3.8	10.0	26.0	35.8	54.9	63.1
Others	4.7	3.9	3.3	9.3	4.3	1.3	0.6
Total	100.0	100.0	100.0	100.0	100.0	100.0	100.0

SOURCE: Bank of Thailand, *Monthly Bulletin*, various issues.

increases in petroleum prices and the resulting international economic disruptions. The first petroleum price increase in 1973–1974 occurred almost simultaneously with the world commodity boom. Between 1972 and 1974 rising prices for Thailand's major export items—including rice, rubber, tin, and maize—helped offset the effect of the petroleum price increase on the country's balance of payments. Nevertheless, Thailand was by no means immune from the impact of these increases. Inflation rates rose rapidly in 1973 and 1974, and the growth of the economy fell in 1974 and 1975. The decline in economic activity caused great concern to the country's economic policy makers. When domestic inflation fell to around 5 percent, the government started to move toward aggressive measures for economic recovery. These included con-

TABLE 2.5   Share of Exports by Product (percentage)

Product	1958	1963	1968	1973	1978	1983	1987
Rice	46.0	35.4	27.6	11.2	12.6	13.8	7.6
Rubber	20.6	19.7	13.3	14.2	9.7	8.1	6.8
Maize	2.8	8.9	12.0	9.2	5.2	5.8	1.3
Tin	4.0	7.7	11.0	6.3	8.7	3.6	0.8
Tapioca	3.0	4.5	5.6	7.9	13.1	10.5	6.9
Teak	3.7	1.4	1.2	1.3	0.3	—	—
Wood products	—	0.1	0.1	1.4	1.2	0.9	1.2
Sugar	—	1.3	—	3.6	4.8	4.3	2.9
Shrimp	—	0.5	2.0	2.5	1.8	2.2	1.9
Mung bean	0.4	0.6	1.0	1.2	1.4	1.1	0.5
Jute and kenaf	1.1	0.7	4.9	3.3	0.5	0.8	0.6
Tungsten	0.1	—	0.3	0.8	1.2	0.1	—
Fluorite	—	0.1	0.8	0.7	0.2	0.2	0.1
Textile products	—	—	—	2.1	8.3	10.0	16.2
Jewelry	—	—	—	—	2.5	4.9	6.6
Tobacco leaves	1.3	0.4	1.5	1.0	1.4	1.2	0.4
Integrated circuits	—	—	—	—	2.6	4.0	5.1
Canned pineapple	—	—	—	—	1.4	1.3	1.2
Cement	0.2	0.6	0.1	1.0	—	—	—
Other exports	16.8	15.1	18.6	32.3	23.1	27.2	39.9
Total exports	100.0	100.0	100.0	100.0	100.0	100.0	100.0

SOURCE: Bank of Thailand, *Monthly Bulletin*, various issues.

trolling prices of essential products (including petroleum), relaxing credit control, and increasing public expenditures and social services. Domestic economic activities soon recovered, along with the world economic recovery. Real GDP growth averaged 9 percent annually in the period 1975–1978, with an average real manufacturing growth rate of 12.5 percent annually.

Thailand was hit harder by the second petroleum price increase and subsequent worldwide recession. The country had become more dependent on external trade, and barter terms of trade were unfavorable. The balance of payments was in deficit, and inflation was much higher than in the years after the first petroleum price increase. The consumer price index rose by 7 to 10 percent between 1977 and 1979, and climbed to 19.7 percent in 1980.

While the performance of Thailand's industrial sector in the 1970s was quite respectable, economic growth was partly financed by increased foreign borrowing. This led to a heavy debt-servicing burden in later years. Although gross investment remained high, at about a quarter of GDP for the decade, the savings-investment gap widened from a surplus of 0.7 percent of GDP in the period 1971–1975 to a deficit of 3.8

percent of GDP in the period 1976–1980. The government fiscal deficit increased substantially from 1.7 percent of GDP in the period 1971–1975 to around 5 percent of GDP in the period 1976–1980. The public-sector deficit and the unfavorable international balances of trade and payments were aggravated in the early 1980s, and austerity measures were adopted. These measures resulted in slower overall growth and substantially slower industrial growth during the first half of the 1980s.

The economic situation in the 1980s. Average annual real GDP growth between 1980 and 1986 averaged only 5.5 percent, with the average manufacturing rate falling to 5.4 percent. Externally, Thailand was confronted with deteriorating barter terms of trade due to depressed export commodity prices and increased petroleum prices. The trade deficit rose to 7 percent of GDP in the period 1980–1985, and the debt-service ratio jumped to 21.9 percent in 1985. Internally, the large budget deficit and rapid public debt accumulation since the mid-1970s constrained the government's ability to finance economic expansion. In 1983, for the first time in more than a decade, the value of exports was lower than in the previous year, while the value of imports grew significantly; this combination led to a large trade deficit of almost 90 billion baht. The Thai baht was largely tied to the U.S. dollar, and as the value of the U.S. dollar rose substantially in the first half of the 1980s, the competitiveness of Thai exports was eroded. The baht was devalued twice in 1981 (by a total of around 10 percent) and once in 1984 (by around 15 percent). The 1984 devaluation was linked to a change in the exchange rate system that tied the baht to a basket of currencies instead of solely to the U.S. dollar.

Since 1986, however, there has been a marked turnaround in economic growth. Although in 1986 real economic growth was rather low at 4.7 percent, a decline in the price of petroleum contributed to an improved balance-of-payments situation and price stability. The trade deficit was drastically reduced to 14.4 billion baht in 1986, about one-fourth of the 1985 level. This improvement was due to high growth in exports together with a fall in the cost of imports. In 1987 the economy showed it was clearly recovering, with real GDP growth at 8 percent. Merchandise exports rose by 29 percent, with manufactured exports making the largest contribution to export growth. In response to a rapid increase in demand for investment and consumer goods, however, imports grew at an even higher rate of 39 percent, and the trade deficit rose to 44 billion baht. This trade deficit was partly offset by increased foreign-exchange income from tourism and other services, which led to a current-account deficit of 19.4 billion baht—only 1.5 percent of GDP. In 1988 growth was accelerating to a projected 10.5 percent, a level that has negative current account implications.

The economic recovery of 1987 was made possible by several factors. In addition to the increase in export demand, domestic demand picked up substantially after two years of recession. Several rounds of downward adjustment in interest rates, petroleum prices, and utility prices, together with active promotion of investment and tourism, have helped to boost domestic economic activity. The change in the value of major currencies and more flexible management of the baht since the 1984 devaluation have enabled Thailand to increase exports of goods and services. Economic recovery has also helped the government to strengthen its financial position. The country's debt-service ratio was reduced from 21.9 percent in 1985 to 17 percent in 1987. The government's fiscal position has improved as tax revenues increased with economic recovery.

Since the mid-1980s manufacturing has emerged as the largest sector of the Thai economy (see Table 2.1), and the proportion of manufactures in total merchandise exports overtook that of agricultural products in 1985 (see Table 2.4). There has also been diversification in the products exported: Table 2.5 shows that the number of principal export items (defined to be export items that exceed 1 percent of total export value) and the proportion of "other exports" have increased steadily over time.

In the 1980s foreign direct investment flows to Thailand increased rapidly, with a significant proportion of such investment going to the manufacturing sector (see Table 2.6). Japanese investment in particular has risen rapidly since 1985. Investment from Asian newly industrializing countries, particularly Taiwan, also increased considerably. Unlike the 1960s and 1970s, when foreign investment was mainly in import-substituting industries, recent foreign investment has been mostly in export industries. Increased foreign investment has thus contributed to export expansion.

Policy Reforms

Economic policy framework. The economic policy framework in Thailand discussed here refers mainly to macroeconomic policies that have an impact on production and trade, as well as trade and industrial policies. Macroeconomic policies begin with an overall objective of economic development in terms of economic growth, financial stability, and social equity, with the emphasis varying at different times. These objectives are translated into policy variables in the form of fiscal and monetary policies as outlined in a series of economic and social development plans starting from 1960, each plan covering a period of five years. At present, Thailand is in the midst of the sixth plan, 1987–1991.

TABLE 2.6   Net Private Foreign Direct Investment by Industry (million baht)

Industry	1971–1975	1976–1980	1981–1985	1986	1987
Financial institutions	2,015.9	(136.3)	10.2	510.2	(3,839.3)
Trade	1,854.3	2,170.9	5,789.7	1,777.5	842.4
Construction	936.0	1,644.1	5,400.3	1,234.9	1,349.1
Mining and quarrying	1,508.4	990.9	7,207.1	240.2	192.0
Oil exploration	1,396.3	713.4	6,446.9	236.4	251.3
Others	112.1	277.5	760.2	3.8	(59.3)
Agriculture	27.2	196.6	215.7	199.8	289.6
Industry	2,640.6	3,319.5	1,0813.4	2,136.8	4,709.9
Food	364.2	251.9	607.3	284.2	395.8
Textiles	1,216.5	688.0	889.8	85.0	996.9
Metal and nonmetallic	162.5	120.8	1,246.3	(36.0)	365.1
Electrical appliances	332.9	1,245.2	3,010.3	617.0	1,136.5
Machinery and transport equipment	52.7	345.5	930.4	14.9	159.9
Chemicals	295.0	487.5	1,406.0	484.0	868.1
Petroleum products	61.3	56.7	2,052.0	8.2	(15.8)
Construction materials	53.3	(123.9)	84.3	5.4	11.0
Others	102.2	247.8	587.0	674.1	792.4
Services	439.2	1,466.8	3,460.5	810.6	1,167.8
Transportation and travel	187.8	850.5	1,178.6	255.6	220.6
Housing and real estate	91.3	200.5	505.1	39.9	320.0
Hotels and restaurants	93.3	92.1	580.1	100.3	99.6
Others	66.8	323.7	1,196.7	414.8	527.6
Total	9,421.6	9,652.5	32,896.9	6910.0	4,711.5

SOURCE: Bank of Thailand.

Policies on production and trade of industrial goods include investment promotional incentives, production permits, local content requirements, tariff protection, credit subsidy, import and export control, and trade promotion and negotiations.

Content and sequencing of reform. Since 1960 macroeconomic, trade, and industrial policies have undergone a series of changes. These changes were minor policy adjustments, except for the second half of the 1980s when policy changes could be considered as reforms. Even then the major changes were more in terms of macroeconomic policies than trade and industrial policies.

The performance of the Thai economy has corresponded well with the macroeconomic policies of different periods. During the first and second plans, covering the period 1961 to 1972, the policies were to promote economic growth by means of government expenditure. At that time the world economy was experiencing high economic growth and financial stability. The Thai economy registered a high average growth rate of 7 percent, with practically no inflation. Industrial and trade policies at this time were designed to promote high growth in production for domestic sales. Tariff protection and investment-promoting tax incentives were provided. In response to macroeconomic stimulation and protection, the industrial sector grew rapidly, producing mainly import substitutes.

The industrial strategy started in the 1960s was continued into the 1970s. The first petroleum price increase created instability in the economy; fortunately this was followed by a period of commodity boom. There was, therefore, no real need to restrict imports and boost exports. Nevertheless, a number of measures, such as tax rebates and refunds, were introduced to promote manufactured exports. Industrial policy at this time was becoming neutral, but still favored the domestic market. In fact, tariff protection for domestic industries increased between 1974 and 1978 (Narongchai 1980). Furthermore, macroeconomic policies, especially exchange-rate policy, were not intended to promote exports.

The petroleum price increases of 1979 and 1980 brought Thailand a series of economic crises, which eventually led to major economic policy reforms in the mid-1980s. The reforms drastically affected the pattern of trade and industrial production.

The huge increase in the petroleum import bill, which was 40 percent of the total import bill in 1982, meant that the government had to borrow heavily abroad. This increase happened when the value of the U.S. dollar—and hence the baht—was very high, which increased the incentive to import. So by 1983 the current-account deficit and the debt-service ratio were both rising at alarming rates. The situation eventually forced the government to devalue the baht and tie it to a basket of currencies. Since then, exchange-rate policy has deliberately favored exports. For example, when the U.S. dollar started to depreciate vis-à-vis other major currencies, especially the Japanese yen and the deutsche mark, the baht was allowed to fall with the U.S. dollar for almost two years.

The economic crises of the early 1980s led to two other major policy changes. First, the private sector was given much more recognition as an engine of economic recovery. The government was encouraging the private sector to play a leading role in investment, arguing that the public sector was too restricted financially. Business practices were liberalized to allow the private sector to take full advantage of market opportunities. Second, industrial policy emphasized export production much more than it had previously. Investment-promotion schemes and activities were designed to encourage production for export. There was a renewed effort at export promotion by the Ministry of Commerce. The Finance Ministry streamlined the tax rebate and refund schemes and made some changes in the tariff structure since it was still biased in favor of import-competing industries (see Industrial Management Corporation 1985).

These policy changes, as well as changes in the world economy, had a better-than-expected impact on the Thai economy. Private investment from domestic and foreign sources, especially in manufactured exports, started to rise in 1986 and has accelerated rapidly since then. The composition of exports has changed drastically, with the proportion of manufactured goods increasing greatly. Much of the credit for these impressive changes has been given to the policy reforms introduced in the mid-1980s.

Policy Decision Making and the Role of Research

The decision-making process. Until 1988 the most common form of government in Thailand consisted of a military leadership supported by civilian technocrats and bureaucrats. The civilian technocrats played a very important role in shaping the content of economic policies. There was a brief period of elected government in the 1970s, and in the 1980–1988 period elected politicians played a more important role in the power structure. Since August 1988, Thailand has been run by an almost entirely elected government.

During the 1960s the prime minister and his cabinet made all of the major economic decisions. The National Economic and Social Development Board (NESDB), the Bank of Thailand, and the Fiscal Policy Office of the Ministry of Finance played important roles as far as macroeconomic issues were concerned. Sectoral policies involved mainly the line ministries. Usually these agencies submitted their proposals to the cabinet for final decision. The decision-making process was not open, and there was no coordination between government agencies.

In the 1970s economic management in Thailand went through several changes. In 1974 and 1975 a group of advisers, who were mainly academics, led by the prominent technocrat Dr. Puey Ungphakorn, was very influential in the decision-making process and prepared many decisions for the cabinet. Unfortunately, political disturbances in the second half of the 1970s confused the entire economic decision-making process until 1981, when the first government of Prime Minister Prem Tinnasulanonda restored and improved it.

Prime Minister Prem was in power for eight years, with five cabinets. The decision-making process did not change very much during this time. Prime Minister Prem appointed a number of technocrats to his cabinet, set up the economic cabinet, strengthened the Office of the Secretariat to the Prime Minister, and appointed a few prominent academics as his advisers. These people made the economic decisions. They were open to advice from outside, both domestic and foreign, and to members of the media. They also coordinated the numerous line ministries. The economic decision-making process during this period was stable and predictable.

Since August 1988 the economic decision-making process has become less centralized and less coordinated. The prime minister still holds the greatest influence, but individual line ministers are influential in their areas of responsibility. The prime minister relies on independent advisers and in some cases overrules proposals of line ministries, but there is no longer a central body. The role of the NESDB is in long-term policy, and the Office of the Secretariat to the Prime Minister serves more like a secretary than a secretariat.

Sources of policy information. This section covers the period since 1981, when many policy reforms were implemented during the various governments of Prime Minister Prem.

Internal government agencies. The three agencies that were most influential in policy reforms were the Bank of Thailand, the Fiscal Policy Office of the Ministry of Finance, and the NESDB. The first two were involved mainly in macroeconomic policies, while the NESDB was active in both macroeconomic and sectoral policies. The Fiscal Policy Office was responsible for work on tariff policy, and the Board of Investment provided inputs to the government on investment-promotion policy. Each of these agencies has some policy-research capability, especially the Bank of Thailand and the NESDB; they have research units but not separate research institutes.

External agencies. When policy changes were contemplated, the NESDB, the Fiscal Policy Office, and the Board of Investment made use of outside agencies. Local consultants were used, the most prominent being consultants organized by the Industrial Management Company, a subsidiary of the Industrial Finance Corporation of Thailand. The Industrial Management Company was commissioned to carry out studies on structural adjustment of the industrial sector, reform of investment incentives, and energy conservation. In addition, the company was commissioned by the United Nations Industrial Development Organization and the World Bank to carry out a number of other policy studies in connection with industry and trade policy reforms for the benefit of the government. The Industrial Management Company collaborated with foreign consultants from Australia and Canada in its series of policy studies. Government agencies also benefited from the work of a number of foreign consultants and policy researchers commissioned by the World Bank. As for independent research institutions, only the Thailand Development Research Institute played a significant role, but mainly on macroeconomic policies. Finally, certain individual academics who served as advisers to the prime minister had strong input into the decision-making process.

The policy research transmission system. The transmission system was based on confidential relationships between government agencies and researchers rather than on open public debate. Because research work was commissioned mainly by policy agencies, the initial step was the submission of reports by researchers to contracting agencies. The agencies then prepared policy proposals for submission to the cabinet and the prime minister. The usual forum at that time was the Council of Economic Ministers, known as the economic cabinet, to which the NESDB was the secretariat. Sometimes researchers were invited to make an oral presentation to economic cabinet meetings or a specialized subcommittee appointed by the government. Under Prime Minister Prem the government was very open to public debate on policy issues, and indeed the public responded by being very active in policy discussion. Coverage of economic issues in the mass media began at this time and since then has expanded to a number of newspapers, magazines, and television programs. In general the public was in favor of a more liberal and competitive economic system and supported the government's export-oriented policies and promotion of foreign investment.

Policy research in public decision making. It is not possible to say to what extent policy research was used in public decision making on macroeconomic policy and trade and industry reform under Prime Minister Prem. Certain key individuals, however, were included in policy decisions, and some of them were involved in or had access to policy research.

As mentioned earlier, the main thrust of the trade and industry reform was through macroeconomic policy rather than sectoral policy. Research on macroeconomic policy was carried out by the Bank of Thailand, the Fiscal Policy Office of the Ministry of Finance, the NESDB, and the Thailand Development Research Institute, which also made use of university researchers. Among these, the work of government agencies has had more influence. In the case of sectoral policy, however, there was more reliance on research outside government agencies. Perhaps this was part of the reason why sectoral policy was less influential than macroeconomic policy in Thailand.

In order to enhance the role of policy research in a country like Thailand, it is necessary to ensure high quality research work and have a practical transmission mechanism. This implies strong and independent research institutes, strong government research agencies, and close collaboration between them all.

Independent research institutes can mobilize expertise from domestic and foreign sources and organize public debates on policy issues to influence and create public opinion. Collaboration between independent research institutes and government research agencies will ensure that policy recommendations consider issues of practicality. In Thailand policy makers who make use of research rely on that of government agencies. This situation may be changing slightly, as more policy makers want to have inputs from independent research agencies. In any case, the desirability and the practicality of collaboration between government and independent agencies remains.

MANAGING TRADE AND INDUSTRY REFORMS IN MALAYSIA

The Malaysian economy has undergone significant structural changes since independence in 1957. The economy has been transformed from essentially primary producing in the 1950s to rapidly industrializing in the 1980s. The export-oriented industrialization strategy of the 1970s was preceded by an import-substitution phase. Further industrialization based on a second round of import substitution was initiated in the early 1980s, and the proportion of manufactures in total exports has increased.

Malaysia has a structured administrative system under a federal government. Policies pass through the administrative hierarchy before they reach the cabinet, the highest policy-making body in the country. The Economic Planning Unit, the Treasury, and the central bank provide inputs for policy formulation.

Although Malaysia has relied heavily on foreign consultants in the past, their role has decreased. Malaysian academics, who are regarded as living in an ivory tower and not relating to the realities of the world, have had a poor rapport with the government. Consequently, a lot of valuable academic research work has been ignored by policy makers, and academics have been discouraged by the sensitivity of policy makers to public criticism.

More often than not, public debate takes place after policy announcements, seldom before them. There are important exceptions, however, such as the annual prebudget dialogues conducted by the

Finance Ministry and the policy work of the National Economic Consultative Council established in January 1989.

To play a constructive role in the policy process, academic researchers need to provide a range of policy options with the costs and benefits of each option clearly spelled out. At present there are few incentives for academics to do this, since academic success is measured largely in terms of publications in international journals.

The effects of trade and industrial policies on the Malaysian economy are not the subject of the present inquiry. The principal concerns of this chapter are the substance and the process of trade and industry reforms, as well as the process aspect of reforms, which provide an insight into the mechanics of policy formulation in Malaysia. An attempt is made to go behind Malaysia's trade and industrial policies with two main objectives in mind: (1) to explain the rationale for and the circumstances surrounding major policy shifts, and (2) to examine the process through which policy decisions are arrived at and implemented.

First, this chapter analyzes Malaysia's industrial structure and the policy variables behind the industrial restructuring that took place from the 1960s through the 1980s. Second, the chapter focuses on Malaysia's trade regime, with particular reference to trade liberalization. Then the major policy actions undertaken by the Malaysian authorities are discussed, followed by an analysis of the policy process. Finally, some policy inferences are drawn from the preceding analysis.

Industrial Restructuring

Since Malaysia's independence in 1957, the economy has undergone major changes. From primary production in the 1950s, it has gone to rapid industrialization in the 1980s. There are signs that Malaysia will join the newly industrializing countries before the end of the 1990s. The share of the primary sector in gross domestic product (GDP) declined from 46 percent in 1957 to 33 percent in 1987, while that of the secondary sector increased from 6 percent to 11 percent during the same period.

Import substitution. After independence, industrialization began with a low-key phase of import substitution in the 1960s. In the early stages, the new industries concentrated mainly on the manufacture of consumer goods for which there was a home market. During the import-substitution phase, the contribution of the manufacturing sector to the country's GDP increased from 11 percent in 1957 to 13 percent in 1968, and manufacturing's share of total employment increased from 6 percent to 9 percent. The growth of manufacturing output was particularly rapid in the initial years, mainly caused by low base values. It began to slow down soon after, as the domestic market neared saturation.

It was also clear that import substitution could not effectively solve unemployment. The generous investment incentives had clearly favored capital-intensive operations by subsidizing the price of capital, resulting in low labor absorption. The contributions of the various manufacturing groups to value added and employment did not change markedly in the period 1963–1968 (Fong 1985). The manufacturing sector did not experience substantial structural changes during the latter part of the import-substitution phase, with food, rubber products, and wood products dominating the sector's contributions to both value added and employment.

Export orientation. After 1968 there was a policy switch from import substitution to export promotion. Nevertheless, the new export strategy did not mean the abandonment of import substitution. Instead of withdrawing its support for inward-looking industries the government pursued its export orientation and import substitution simultaneously.

The performance of the industrial sector after the policy reorientation was impressive. The share of manufacturing in GDP increased from 13 percent in 1968 to 23 percent in 1987. In absolute terms, manufacturing output multiplied from M$1.1 billion in 1968 to M$13.7 billion in 1987. The share of manufacturing employment rose from 9 percent in 1968 to 18 percent in 1987, with the number of jobs in the manufacturing sector increasing fourfold.

Significant industrial restructuring took place in the 1970s. In 1968 the major industries, by value added, were food manufacturing, rubber products, and wood products. By the mid-1970s the electronics and electrical industry, the garment and textile industry, and food manufacturing all saw increases in exports.

Export-oriented industries tend to have a higher employment effect than import-substituting ones. Employment coefficients for the export-processing zones exceed those for manufactured exports as a whole. The coefficients are also higher for total manufactured exports than for total manufacturing production (Verbruggen 1984).

Heavy industries. In the 1980s heavy industrialization in Malaysia was based on two main considerations. First, export-oriented industries in export-processing zones seemed too footloose and insufficiently linked to the domestic economy to have a lasting impact. Second, heavy industry was seen as the logical step toward an advanced stage of industrialization after import substitution and export orientation. The Republic of Korea had a demonstration effect on Malaysia.

The launching of the Heavy Industries Corporation of Malaysia by the Malaysian government marked the beginning of the heavy industrialization program in the country and manifested the active government participation and intervention in the country's industrial development. The corporation became involved in those industries that were based on domestic resources, namely, petroleum and gas. The 1982 official estimates of reserves were 2.3 billion barrels of petroleum and 48 billion cubic feet of natural gas.

Six steel mills operate in Malaysia, the largest being the Hicom-Perwaja steel mill with an annual production capacity of 615,000 tons. Given current world prices, domestic steel production is not commercially viable. The domestic market is too small to absorb all output, and exporting is difficult, as the product is not price competitive unless it is subsidized.

National car manufacturing began in 1985. In the first year of production, output was 7,500 units and was projected to reach 105,100 by 1988. In the face of the slow growth of domestic demand for passenger cars and the difficulties of the export market, the national car plant finds its output targets unrealistic. It appears that the plant must produce at least 100,000 units a year just to break even.

Small-scale industries. Small-scale industries, defined as those with fewer than fifty workers, account for nearly three-fourths of all manufacturing establishments in Malaysia. The majority employ fewer than five workers. Small industry units employ more workers per unit of capital, creating substantial employment opportunities and thus are labor intensive and capital saving. On the average, the fixed capital per worker in small industries is about 12 percent lower than that for large industries (Chee 1986). Small industries, by creating a large number of low-wage jobs, produce relatively small increases in income for a large number of people. Through subcontracting, small industries are important complements to large firms.

Small-scale industries, unlike large-scale industries, have not received much government support. In theory they have received some attention in the various five-year development plans since 1966. Although several specific measures were undertaken to support them, the structure of investment incentives remained biased in favor of large, capital-intensive enterprises.

Conscious of the discriminatory nature of the investment incentives system, the Malaysian government has tried to redress the imbalance by offering special privileges through annual budgets. But the various forms of assistance given to small industries have been piecemeal or ad hoc. A comprehensive national policy toward small industries is lacking. It has become obvious that large-scale industries alone cannot solve the unemployment problem in the country. Despite the 4.7 percent real

GDP growth in 1987 and the estimated 8.2 percent real GDP growth for 1988, unemployment remains high at about 8.5 percent. The government is therefore turning its attention to small and medium-sized industries with relatively high labor-capital ratios.

The Trade Regime

The importance of trade and hence trade policies to the Malaysian economy can hardly be overemphasized. Exports account for over one-half of Malaysia's gross national product (GNP).

Trade profile. The composition of Malaysia's exports and imports has changed dramatically, reflecting the pace and character of industrialization. Thus, the share of raw materials (Standard International Trade Classification) in total exports has declined from 54 percent in 1970 to 24 percent in 1987, although in absolute terms these exports have nearly quadrupled. In contrast, the share of manufactures (SITC 5–8) in total exports has increased sharply, from 28 percent in 1970 to 42 percent in 1987.

The pattern of Malaysia's imports has also changed markedly over the years. The ratio of food, beverages, and tobacco to total imports fell from 21 percent to 10 percent between 1970 and 1987. The proportion of manufactures (SITC 5–8) in total imports, on the other hand, rose from 58 percent to 77 percent during the same period.

The direction of trade flows has not changed greatly over the years. The United States, Japan, and the European Community continue to dominate Malaysia's exports and imports. The combined share of the United States, Japan, and the European Community in Malaysia's exports has remained stable at 51 percent from 1970 to 1987, while their aggregate share in Malaysia's imports has increased from 51 percent to 54 percent during the same period. The United States accounts for a growing share of exports and imports, while the role of the European Community as a trading partner seems to be declining.

Singapore is another major trading partner, accounting for 75 percent of Malaysia's exports to the Association of Southeast Asian Nations (ASEAN) and 71 percent of Malaysia's imports from ASEAN in 1987. Singapore ranks second as an export destination and third as an import source for Malaysia.

Structure of protection. Malaysia's industrialization program has been supported by protection, but the degree of protection accorded to domestic industries was relatively low by developing country standards.

Malaysia's protection system has undergone substantial changes in both nominal and effective terms. The average nominal protection rate for manufactures as a whole increased from 13 percent in 1965 (Power 1971) to 18 percent in 1970 (Ariff 1975) and to 22 percent in 1978 (Lee 1985). The average effective protection rate increased from 4 percent in 1965 (Power 1971) to 44 percent in 1970 (Ariff 1975) and to 55 percent in 1973 before declining to 39 percent in 1978 (Lee 1985).

There have also been changes in the structure of protection. The proportion of industries receiving nominal protection rates of less than 40 percent declined from 92 percent to 88 percent between 1970 and 1978. Nominal rates for all major product groups increased between 1965 and 1978, but the pattern of tariff escalation changed very little over this period.

Changes in the structure of effective protection were more marked. In 1965, 39 percent of manufacturing industries had negative effective protection rates; this was reduced to 31 percent in 1970 and further to 14 percent in 1978. At the same time the proportion of industries enjoying effective protection rates of more than 100 percent increased from 8 percent in 1965 to 16 percent in 1970 before falling to 10 percent in 1978. There has been wide dispersion in both nominal and effective rates. The coefficients of variation in nominal protection rates show no clear trend; by contrast, effective protection rates show a clear downward trend in dispersion with the coefficient of variation falling from 102 in 1963 to 60 in 1973, and a marginal increase to 64 in 1978 (Lee 1985).

There have also been marked changes in the effective protection rates by major product categories: rates for consumer durables increased sharply from –5 percent in 1965 to 173 percent in 1978, nondurable consumer goods ranked second in 1978, and intermediate products have tended to receive even lower effective protection rates. A more serious observation is that the structure of protection has produced an anti-export bias. Several export activities suffer from negative effective protection. Even for those industries with positive rates, the anti-export bias tends to be strong, as the value added for export sales at world prices is often less than that for domestic sales.

It is quite clear that the structure of protection in Malaysia is incompatible with a strategy of export-oriented industrialization. An industrial policy cannot pursue import substitution and export orientation simultaneously. The anti-export bias has been mitigated to some extent by offsetting duty exemptions and by incentives such as export allowances. It would be preferable if tariff distortions were removed instead of being offset in this manner.

Policy Framework

Malaysian governments have been very active in industrial policy.

Investment incentives. Successive governments have relied heavily on tax incentives to foster industrialization. Immediately after independence in 1957, the government mounted an industrialization program based on import substitution, with the twin objectives of creating employment and diversifying the economy. The central instrument was the Pioneer Industries (Relief from Income Tax) Ordinance of 1958. The ordinance granted tax holidays to manufacturing establishments with pioneer status. Pioneer industries were given an initial tax relief of between two and five years, depending on the size of the capital. The Pioneer Industries Ordinance of 1958 was superseded by the Investment Incentives Act of 1968, which marked a major shift in the industrialization strategy from import substitution toward export orientation. The 1968 act still maintained tax holidays as the principal instrument.

Income tax relief was given to pioneer firms, depending on capital size, product produced, industry location, and domestic content. The 1968 act also allowed pioneer firms to carry forward net losses incurred during the pioneer period so that it could be offset against assessable tax in the post–pioneer period. The 1968 act provided investment tax credits to approved projects. Tax credits could amount to no less than 25 percent of the capital expenditure within five years after approval, and the rate was stretched to a maximum of 40 percent for firms operating in "development areas," producing "priority products," and utilizing at least 50 percent local content.

To encourage production for export, the 1968 act offered several incentives, including double deduction of export promotional expenses from taxable income, accelerated depreciation, and an export allowance.

The sluggish inflow of foreign investments in the mid-1980s led to the major redesign of the investment incentives system in the Promotion of Investments Act 1986. Under the new act, pioneer status was limited to companies participating in promoted activities or producing promoted products. (The list of promoted activities or promoted products has been gazetted, Gazette Notification P.U. (A) 391, 11 November 1986.) The 1986 act provides tax relief to companies with pioneer status for five years; the tax relief period is extended to ten years for companies that invest an additional M$25 million or employ five hundred full-time Malaysian workers at the end of the five-year tax-relief period or meet any criteria to be determined by the ministers so as to promote or enhance the economic and technological development of the country.

The 1986 act also provides for abatement of adjusted income to manufacturing units operating in promoted industrial areas, to small-scale manufacturing companies, and to all companies that comply with government policy on equity participation and employment.

A major incentive embodied in the 1986 act is the investment tax allowance. The investment tax allowance rates for the manufacturing sector vary up to a maximum of 100 percent, depending primarily on the proportion of products exported. Other export incentives provided by the Promotion of Investments Act 1986 include export allowances, double deduction of overseas promotional expenses, and double deduction of export credit insurance premiums.

To encourage research and development activities, the 1986 act includes double deduction of research expenditure approved by the finance minister and capital allowance for plant and machinery used for purposes of approved research.

Tariffs. Prior to independence tariffs were mainly for revenue. In 1959 the tariff schedule was reclassified. Commonwealth preferential margins were eliminated for several import items and abolished altogether in 1967. The Tariff Advisory Committee was established to award tariff protection to pioneer industries. By the end of 1962, about twenty-five pioneer industry products received tariff protection (Tan 1973). In 1962 the Tariff Advisory Committee was replaced by the Tariff Advisory Board, which had imposed modest protective duties on more than two hundred imported items by 1963 (Power 1971). By 1963 tariffs averaged 15 percent, but many items had no tariffs (Wheelright 1965). Tariffs were raised in many cases and extended to several more items after 1965. On the whole Malaysian tariff rates remained low in comparison with other developing countries.

Separate tariff structures exist for Peninsular Malaysia, Sabah, and Sarawak. Tariff rates for a large number of goods were harmonized with the establishment of a single customs area in 1967 (Customs Duties [Exemption] [Goods of Malaysian Origin] Order 1965 and Customs [Malaysian Common Tariffs] Order 1967). The Tariff Advisory Board, which had held open hearings, was replaced by the Federal Industrial Development Authority (now called the Malaysian Industrial Development Authority).

The Customs (Dumping and Subsidies) Ordinance 1959 gives protection to Malaysian manufactures against dumping. The most significant aspect of the ordinance was the power given to the Minister of Commerce and Industry to impose interim duties as soon as a prima facie case of dumping had been established.

The Malaysian authorities have successfully resisted attempts by vested interests to raise the tariff rates. The only exceptions to this are the tariffs relating to products competing with those of the local heavy industries, such as iron and steel.

The structure of tariffs is inconsistent with the export-oriented approach subsequently adopted by the government. The built-in bias against exports remains a major factor inhibiting resource allocation in favor of export activities. This led the Malaysian authorities to review the tariff structure. The Economic Planning Unit and the Malaysian Industrial Development Authority have done tariff studies with the help of foreign consultants, but no major tariff reforms have been undertaken. Some tariff cuts have been made in budgets but on an ad hoc basis. There has been no serious attempt at systematic tariff reform. Nevertheless, Malaysia may reduce its tariff rates in the Uruguay round of multilateral trade negotiations.

Export processing zones and licensed manufacturing warehouses (bonded warehouses) are exempt from import duties. Thus imports of machinery, raw materials, and intermediate inputs are duty free if the final outputs are meant for export. Likewise, duty drawbacks are given to other manufacturers producing for the export market provided certain conditions are fulfilled—re-export of imports within twelve months, for example. Duty drawbacks take the form of tax rebates upon re-export.

Preferential tariff cuts have been made within the ASEAN economic cooperation framework. Under the preferential trading arrangement, Malaysia has already reduced its tariffs by 10 to 30 percent on many imports from ASEAN members and by 1992 will reduce them by an across-the-board 50 percent.

Financial incentives. Early in 1979 preshipment preferential export refinancing was introduced. Under this scheme, loans up to 50 percent of export value could be extended to manufacturers at relatively low interest rates. In October 1981 postshipment financing facilities were also introduced. The postshipment facility was aimed at resource based industries and other products with high domestic value added, while the preshipment facility was targeted at exports that were experiencing difficulties in foreign markets due to protectionist barriers, depressed market conditions, and the like.

This scheme, now known as export credit refinancing, is managed by Bank Negara, the central bank. It was redesigned in December 1986. As a result, the preshipment loans have been raised from 50 percent to 80 percent of the value of the export order, and the preshipment facility is extended to trading companies and indirect exporters (domestic suppliers of goods to exporters). The previous M$5 million refinancing ceiling was abolished, leaving the amount of loans to the discretion of commercial banks. At the same time, the minimum amount of refinancing has been reduced from M$20,000 to M$10,000 so as to benefit the smaller firms. All products except those in the negative list are now eligible for this facility.

To assist the development of small-scale industries, the government established the Credit Guarantee Corporation in 1972. Under this scheme, commercial banks are obliged to extend at least 10 percent of their savings deposits as loans to small borrowers, up to M$50,000, at relatively low interest rates. The ceiling was subsequently raised to M$200,000 for bumiputras (ethnic Malays) and M$100,000 for other borrowers.

Regulations. The Malaysian economy is highly regulated, with regulations being looked upon as an important policy instrument. Many regulations revolve around the New Economic Policy. The Industrial Coordination Act represents the single most important piece of legislation affecting the industrial sector. The act, which came into existence in 1975, requires inter alia that all manufacturing companies with a paid-up capital of M$250,000 or more obtain a license from the minister of trade and industry, who is empowered by the act to refuse a license in the national interest. Under the act, the minister may impose any condition (including compliance with the 30 percent bumiputera equity participation) before a license is issued or renewed.

In 1984 the government tightened the Companies Act 1965 by enacting the Companies (Amendment) Bill 1984, which contained seventy-three amendments, one of which calls for the establishment of a panel to administer, supervise, and control mergers and takeovers. Yet another amendment requires companies to disclose substantial share holdings of 5 percent or more, so as to improve the government surveillance of predatory moves.

Although government regulations are not meant to stifle private sector activities, there are areas of some concern. In particular these include the wide ranging powers of both the minister of trade and industry and the registrar of companies and also the functions of the panel on mergers and takeovers, whose decisions are final and cannot be challenged in a court of law.

The system of regulation has profound implications for the business environment. Its very complexity tends to increase uncertainty and unpredictability. The implementation of regulation is entirely arbitrary. Bureaucratic procedures can be extremely frustrating, with lengthy delays in obtaining official approvals. In fact, the time and resources of private enterprises have been dissipated in circumventing regulations.

The saving grace insofar as regulations are concerned is that Malaysian policy makers are pragmatic people who are prepared to compromise if situations demand it. Thus, the New Economic Policy equity objective of 30 percent bumiputera share has been shelved, at least for the time being, while the Malaysian economy recovers from the 1982–1984 recession. In the same vein, the government has been making serious efforts to cut down bureaucratic barriers. For instance, a one-stop licensing house has been set up at the Ministry of Trade and Industry to handle all manufacturing licenses. The aim is to expedite the processing of all applications so that decisions are arrived at within six weeks. Similarly, the state economic development corporations are simplifying procedures so that the time taken for approval of factory sites will not exceed one month. The extent to which Malaysian policy makers are willing to deregulate is perhaps exemplified by the recent amendments to the National Land Code, which permitted foreign ownership of land.

Privatization. Public enterprises have been the main vehicle for direct government involvement in the economy. The outstanding examples of government direct involvement in trade and industry are Perbadanan Nasional (PERNAS) and the Heavy Industry Corporation of Malaysia. It is now common knowledge that many public enterprises have failed to perform and have incurred heavy losses. With the severe budgetary constraints of the mid-1980s, the burden of public enterprises became too heavy for the government to bear. Hence, privatization of public enterprises became a policy option.

In the period 1984–1985 it was announced that a number of public sector activities would be privatized. Privatization can take any of the following forms:

- conversion of a public enterprise into a private one with 100 percent government equity, as in the case of telecommunications

- partial divestment by the government through sale of its shares, as in the case of Malaysia Airlines

- complete takeover by the private sector, as in the case of aircraft maintenance

- entry of private enterprise into activities that were government monopolies, as in the case of TV3, a private television network

In the present context of trade and industry reforms, the privatization drive has not had much direct impact. For instance, there is not yet a plan to privatize the Heavy Industries Corporation of Malaysia. It is extremely unlikely that there would be any takers even if it were to be privatized, given the serious doubts about its commercial viability.

Exchange-rate policy. The Malaysian ringgit has been tied to a basket of unspecified currencies since September 1975. The exchange-rate policy up to 1984 was strongly linked with the U.S. dollar and the Singapore dollar, resulting in the overvaluation of the ringgit. This tended to penalize exports. The balance-of-payments difficulties of the early

1980s were partly caused by the overvalued Malaysian currency. It has been estimated that by the end of 1984 the exchange rate was overvalued by as much as 20 percent (Semudram 1985).

It became increasingly clear that ringgit overvaluation was hurting the Malaysian economy. Economic activity was sluggish and the balance-of-payments deficit was growing. In the third quarter of 1984, the authorities adopted a more flexible exchange-rate management policy, partly in response to IMF advice.

Central bank intervention in the foreign-exchange market has become intense, in terms of both frequency and magnitude. It has been acting against destabilizing speculation, leaving market forces to determine the equilibrium rate. There are clear indications that the depreciating ringgit has helped Malaysian exports in general and manufactured exports in particular; the external payments deficit has been converted to a substantial surplus.

The Industrial Master Plan. The Industrial Master Plan, released in February 1986, is a blueprint that places high expectations on the manufacturing sector. The plan covers the period 1986–1995 and consists of twenty-two reports. It envisages an annual GDP growth of 6.4 percent during the plan period, with total investment expanding at the rate of 5.7 percent annually. The plan targets a real annual growth rate of 8.8 percent for the manufacturing sector. It also aims to create 705,400 new jobs, which would bring the total number of workers in the manufacturing sector to 1.5 million by 1995.

The Industrial Master Plan has identified several industries for special attention. Among these the rubber product industry figures prominently as one of the leading sectors in the expansion of resource-based industries. The plan aims at raising local consumption of rubber and making the industry export-oriented, with the tire industry being accorded priority status. Other industries include downstream palm-oil-based and palm-kernel-oil-based products (e.g., oleochemicals), food processing (e.g., cocoa products and animal feeds), and wood-based industry. It is hoped that all these industries will become major export earners.

At the same time the plan has opted for import-substitution for aluminum, copper, and heavy industries. Products with growth potential in the nonmetallic minerals industry include cement, glass, and ceramics. The plan has underscored the need for a rationalization of the automobile industry so that there will be only three manufacturers by 1995. The rationalization program envisages upgrading of plants and increasing their size.

The plan calls for large-scale manufactured exports to maintain high industrial growth and recommends a strategy based on:

- a free-trade regime applied to all exporters regardless of products

- application of market principles to the choice of activities undertaken by individual firms

- balanced incentives for import substitution and exports

Development plans. Prior to independence, no serious development planning was undertaken. Development plans such as the 1950–1955 development plan for peninsular Malaysia (then known as Malaya), the 1947–1956 Development and Welfare Plan for Sarawak, and the 1959–1964 Development Plan for Sabah were aggregations of various departmental expansion programs or, at best, projections of annual budgets.

Between the political independence of Malaya in 1957 and the formation of Malaysia in 1963, there were two five-year plans. The First Malaya Plan (1956–1960) was based largely on a study undertaken by a World Bank mission (World Bank 1955). The Second Malaya Plan (1961–1965), based on a Harrod-Domar type model, had a well-defined set of objectives ranked in order of priority.

The First Malaysia Plan (1965–1970) was essentially an extension of the preceding plan and had similar policy objectives and planning techniques. It emphasized the role of the private sector in the development process. The Second Malaysia Plan (1971–1975) was a departure from the previous plans in terms of both objectives and strategies. It was drawn up within the framework of the twenty-year Outline Perspective Plan (1971–1990). Equity considerations were particularly strong in the Second Malaysia Plan. The May 1969 civil disturbances were largely responsible for the launching of the New Economic Policy, which formed the basis of all subsequent five-year plans including the Third Malaysia Plan (1976–1980), Fourth Malaysia Plan (1981–1985), and Fifth Malaysia Plan (1986–1990).

The Policy Process

Tiers of policy formulation. The Malaysian government has a structured administrative system with the federal government in Kuala Lumpur as the apex, and state, district, and kampung (village) constituting the subsystems in the hierarchy. The parliament is constitutionally the supreme body that makes public policy; it has ultimate legislative responsibility. Major policy proposals such as those for industry and trade reforms move through the system to the cabinet (see

Figure 3.1). It is not unusual, as recent experience has shown, for important policies to originate from the prime minister himself, although he obtains the endorsement of the cabinet before implementation.

The civil service occupies a central position in the policy process in terms of evaluation, analysis, periodic reviews and adjustments, and implementation of policies, projects, and programs. The Malaysian civil service has always worked in close cooperation with the political leadership.

Economic planning. Economic planning at the federal level is carried out by a number of institutions including the Economic Planning Unit and the Socioeconomic Research Unit of the Prime Minister's Department, and the planning cells of the Treasury, the central bank, and the various ministries. The ultimate responsibility for planning rests with the cabinet, which is assisted by the National Development Planning Committee, for which the Economic Planning Unit acts as a secretariat. The interagency planning groups, in which the Economic Planning Unit, Treasury, central bank, and Statistics Department are represented, occupy a central position in the planning process, and provide inputs for policy recommendations at the National Development Planning Committee level (see Figure 3.2). In addition, each state has a State Economic Planning Unit, which serves as a secretariat for the State Planning Committee.

Economic planning in Malaysia is only indicative, for the private sector is seen as a major force in economic development. The Economic Planning Unit is responsible to the prime minister, whose backing is absolutely crucial. Development plans are formulated by the unit in consultation with the major decision makers in the public and private sectors. Government agencies and departments are given opportunities to participate in the planning process through proposals for expansion, development, and restructuring.

The Economic Planning Unit, which was established in June 1961, plays a crucial role in the planning process. Its functions range from advising the government on economic problems to drawing up detailed development plans. Its responsibilities include economic analysis, preparation of plans, review and evaluation of projects, and programming and coordination of technical assistance.

The Economic Planning Unit also acts as a secretariat for the National Development Planning Committee, which comprises senior civil servants appointed by the government. This committee not only has a major say in the formulation of development plans, but also undertakes periodic reviews and suggests adjustments in accordance with changing circumstances. Moreover, the committee coordinates the execution of development plans at the center and makes recommendations on resource allocation. While the Economic Planning Unit's focus is on

FIGURE 3.1   Planning, Coordination, and Evaluation

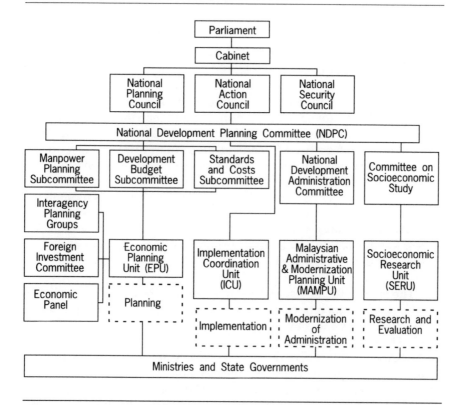

FIGURE 3.2   Planning Process

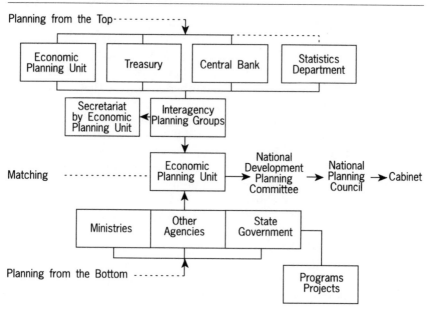

macroeconomic planning, the National Development Planning Committee's main concern is planning at program and project level (Chan 1971).

The implementation of the development plans and the monitoring of progress have proved to be far more difficult than the actual planning itself. The government has adopted an operations room technique (from the military strategy used to combat the communist terrorists during the Emergency years of 1948–1960) to keep a close watch on economic development. Each of the thirteen states has a state operations room, and each district in every state also has a district operations room in the district officer's headquarters. Through its networks linking all the state and district operations rooms, the National Operations Room has full access to information related to the progress of development programs at the state and district levels.

The role of the elites. Malaysian elites may be classified as elected party elites, bureaucratic elites, military elites, and symbolic elites (Tilman 1964). To this list one may add the category of intellectual elites (Naidu 1972). The first category consists essentially of cabinet ministers, members of parliament, members of the state legislative assemblies, and members of the Senate—a group that constitutes the power or primary elite.

The second category comprises the Malaysian civil service. There is considerable collaboration between the top strata of the civil service and the elected party elites, as most of the latter have had some previous civil service experience.

The third category, the military, does not significantly influence economic policy making, but its importance as a stabilizing force should not be underestimated. The political elite has successfully adopted a strategy of appeasement toward the military elite through better pay schemes, promotions, allowances, and other benefits so that the military does not pose any threat (Naidu 1972).

The symbolic elites in Malaysia are the sultans or rulers and the Malay royalty who do not play a direct role in policy making but do act as a legitimizing and stabilizing force. The Conference of Rulers, provided for in the federal constitution, deliberates on national policies on the advice of the prime minister, or chief ministers.

The term intellectual elites refers to specialized elites including academics, business people, scientists, religious leaders, union leaders, and social activists. The intellectuals are often regarded as practitioners of critique. Intellectuals, by definition, are not involved directly in policy making, since one cannot be an objective observer of that in which one also participates. The contribution of the intellectual elites to the development efforts in society may take the form of ideas, suggestions, or criticisms.

Intellectuals influence public policies not only through their journal articles, seminar and conference papers, books, monographs, news features, and so on, but also through their direct involvement as consultants. The latter is only a recent development and its importance should not be overemphasized. By and large, there has been little contact between the government and academia. Local expertise has remained largely untapped by the government. The spasmodic dialogues between academics in universities and policy makers in government are mainly carried out through informal channels and are largely confined to discussions with the lower levels of the government hierarchy.

The perception of the civil service is that academics cannot relate to the practical world. Academics are distrusted in government circles. Instances of academics obtaining information from government departments and passing it on to opposition parties have led to public outcries (Naidu 1972).

The situation, however, is changing. It is no longer rare to find academic involvement in research projects funded by the government. Nevertheless, a lot of valuable research work done by local academics remains unnoticed by policy makers. This is basically a problem of dissemination of research findings, which can be overcome by establishing communication and information networks.

A more serious and difficult problem relates to the hypersensitivity of the key policy makers to public criticisms. The kind of backlash the intellectual elites sometimes receive from the authorities tends to stop open discussion of controversial issues in an intellectual atmosphere. Criticisms of policies are often misconstrued as salvos aimed at the persons responsible for the policies concerned. The problem becomes particularly acute when policy makers are not able to admit that mistakes have been made in the past. It can be very frustrating for the intellectual elite when the system becomes too defensive to permit constructive criticisms.

The Official Secrets Act has an inhibiting effect on research and dissemination of research. The loose definition of an official secret and the stiff mandatory jail sentence for divulging official secrets have made research work hazardous for scholars. Ministers are empowered to add to, delete from, or amend any of the provisions of the official secrets schedule. Further, public officers appointed by a minister or chief minister have the power to classify documents as top secret, confidential, or restricted. University instructors in Malaysia are also affected to some extent by limits imposed on them by the Universities and University Colleges Act. The assurance given by the authorities that no bona fide scholar will be sued under the Official Secrets Act provides no comfort.

Despite this, intellectuals are still free to express their views, but they do not matter much in the policy-making process. The lack of academic debate on practical issues, leading to a diversity of views rather than a focus on areas of agreement, makes the use of academics as advisers difficult.

The role of foreign advisers. Although the role of foreign advisers seems to have dwindled as local expertise develops, the Malaysian government still relies on them, especially in the planning process. The First Malaya Plan was based largely on the recommendations of the World Bank team. All subsequent five-year plans have had some degree of foreign input, albeit decreasing.

Many of the foreign experts in Malaysia were assigned upon request to the various government agencies by international institutions such as the World Bank and the International Monetary Fund. Others were commissioned directly by the Malaysian government to undertake specific projects. Thus, foreign experts have been attached to the Economic Planning Unit and the Malaysian Industrial Development Authority specifically to look into the investment incentives system and the structure of tariff protection. The Industrial Master Plan was largely the work of Korean economists.

Multilateral institutions have played a significant role in bringing about trade and industry reforms in the country. The fact that Malaysia has a low tariff profile may be attributed in no small measure to the advice of the World Bank. The decision to allow the Malaysian ringgit to depreciate in recent times appears to have been made with IMF advice. The role of multilateral institutions in Malaysian policy making should not be overemphasized for two main reasons. First, Malaysian policy makers have always been fairly liberal and pragmatic in their approach, warranting very little external intervention. Second, unlike many other developing countries, Malaysia has never been heavily dependent on the World Bank or the IMF for external funds.

Obviously, there are advantages in employing experts to make policy-making inputs; they may contribute worldwide experience and objectives. They cannot, however, substitute for local experts. They often fail to come to grips with local nuances and realities. Moreover, foreign experts also seemed to have had difficulties in adapting their skills and expertise to the host situation (Yap 1972).

The role of pressure groups. Active pressure groups in Malaysia include consumer associations, environmentalist groups, trade unions, employers' associations, chambers of commerce, and manufacturers' associations. It is difficult to ascertain to what extent they actually influence government policies. It also appears that the opposing interests of these groups tend to neutralize one another. For instance, trade unions and employers' associations often have opposite viewpoints. Likewise, consumer associations and manufacturers' associations tend to offset each other in their demands on tariff protection, for example.

Nevertheless, pressure groups do play a role in the policy process in Malaysia, and the government is sometimes receptive to their ideas and suggestions. The government actively seeks the views of these groups in formulating the annual budgets and five-year plans. The role of trade unions in the policy process was recently manifested in the privatization of telecommunications. The public-sector unions were directly involved in a series of negotiations with the authorities. In spite of all this, Malaysian pressure groups are still in their infancy and are devoid of political power.

The political apparatus. The Malaysian democratic system includes the Dewan Rakyat (house of representatives) and the Dewan Negara (senate). The Yang Dipertuan Agong (the king), who is elected for five years from among the state rulers, is constitutionally the source of all authority, be it legislative, executive, or judicial. The cabinet acts in his name and under his authority. Nevertheless, the king is no more than a constitutional monarch, who must act on the advice of the ministers who form the cabinet.

Members of the Dewan Rakyat are elected. The Dewan Rakyat provides a forum to state and debate government policies. Such debates often take place during question times or adjournment speeches.

The members of the Dewan Negara are either elected by state legislative assemblies (Dewan Undangan Negeri) or appointed by the king. The Dewan Negara is supposed to function as a safety valve that can prevent hasty and ill-considered legislation.

In the Dewan Rakyat, bills are seldom referred to select committees after the first reading; they are debated at the second reading before they are passed at the third reading, if there are no amendments. In practice, there has been very little backbencher participation in the proceedings of the Dewan Rakyat (Jalil 1985; Muzaffar 1985). It is not unusual for government members to stage walkouts when opposition members make adjournment speeches, forcing the Dewan Rakyat to adjourn for lack of a quorum.

Question time at the Dewan Rakyat is sometimes used to secure a change or review of government policies, but usually it is used for party and publicity purposes (Jalil 1985). Question time, however, is one way of ensuring that government is not absolute, but accountable to the people. In practice the government has had no problem in getting its policies endorsed, given the absolute majority in the Dewan Rakyat. The backbencher seldom debates bills tabled by a minister, while adjournment speeches are dominated by the opposition members. It is noteworthy that beginning with the third parliament (1974–1978), the number of questions posed to the minister of trade and industry has increased markedly, but the queries have been generally designed to seek information rather than question government policies.

The debates in the senate have been brief and dull (Jalil 1985). It is not surprising that the senate has been rubber stamping the decisions of Dewan Rakyat, as no members of the opposition parties are admitted to sit in the upper house.

In practice the executive wields considerable power in formulating policies. The Ministry of Trade and Industry is no exception. Policies relating to trade and industry may originate from the minister of trade and industry, or from senior trade officials below, or from the prime minister above. In the final analysis, it is the cabinet that makes the major policy decisions.

Concluding Remarks

The term "reform" connotes major policy improvements based on careful or systematic reviews. There have been no major trade and industry reforms in Malaysia in the strict sense of the term. But there have been important ad hoc policy changes, which have resulted in the changing of gears or the charting of new directions. In this chapter "trade and industry reforms" is loosely defined as encompassing all policies affecting trade and industry, either directly or indirectly.

More often than not, policy changes are first mooted at the ministerial or prime ministerial level before they are seriously considered by various committees comprising senior civil servants. In the process, studies are commissioned before specific projects are implemented. In some cases independent studies by academics and other research institutions influence policies to some extent. But it appears that major policy directions are sometimes decided before the full implications and ramifications are systematically explored through serious studies. Thus, the Look East policy, and the Heavy Industrialization policy were adopted before all the pertinent issues were thoroughly debated. (The Look East policy was aimed at emulating the work ethic of Japanese, Koreans, and Taiwanese, although it was subsequently interpreted to encompass emulation of the trade and industrialization strategies of the East Asian newly industrializing countries.) The danger of this approach is that costly mistakes can be made.

Research has not been part of the local culture; business people, bureaucrats, and politicians make decisions by following their hunches. There are still many who do not fully recognize the value of research. They seem more concerned about the cost of carrying out research than about how much it can contribute.

Economic research can play a useful role in national development by providing basic inputs for decision making. Nevertheless, it cannot thrive in an environment where the policy makers are hypersensitive to criticism. There has been very little rapport between academia and government. The latter is often blamed for not making use of the local talent and for not giving local academics access to data and information in ministries and government agencies. The academics themselves may have to shoulder part of the blame. Their research findings and policy conclusions are published in ways that are not intelligible to policy makers.

All this underscores the need to package research results so that they are usable by policy makers. At present there are no incentives for academics to do this because academic research is motivated primarily by the publish or perish dictum, and academic success calls for publications in international journals. Academics are not interested in preparing papers for the government since they cannot put their names to them and the papers are restricted to internal circulation: they would find it an unrewarding exercise. Seconding of academics to government departments and provisions for spending sabbatical leave on attachment to government departments might be possible.

There is a need to establish a central stock of economic research papers to which policy makers would have ready access. The academic staff of economics faculties in local universities could be required to submit a copy of monographs, articles, and working papers to this stock.

Since there is a lack of public debate on important policy issues prior to policy decisions, the role of academic economists has been one of reacting rather than acting. There are two inherent dangers in this approach. One is that costly errors may be made, and the second is that it tends to create bad feelings between the policy makers and the critics. By contrast, public debate on important issues prior to policy decisions would help policy makers arrive at better decisions and provide academics and others with opportunities to play an active and constructive role.

Traditions are changing, as is demonstrated by the prebudget dialogue the finance minister holds annually. A more recent development is the formation of the National Economic Consultative Council in January 1989 to draft the post-1990 New Economic Policy. It is particularly significant to note that this 150-member council includes representatives from opposition parties, the private sector, academia, and pressure groups, in addition to government officials and members of the ruling party. There is also a move toward greater public sector-private sector interaction in the planning process. The government plans to set up private sector planning groups parallel to the public sector interagency planning groups that play a crucial role in the planning process.

There are signs of improved rapport between the government and academia. Academics are now appointed as panel members of the various expert groups set up by ministries. New research institutions like the Institute of Strategic and International Studies, the Malaysian Institute of Economic Research, and the Institute of Development Studies have emerged. (The Institute of Strategic and International Studies is a think tank funded entirely by the government. It has been acting as a sounding board for major policy issues. Research activities seem to be guided by national interest. The Malaysian Institute of Economic Research is an independent organization set up by private sector interests, but it receives sound financial support from the government. Its focus is on micro- and macroeconomic analysis and monitoring. The Institute of Development Studies is based in Kota Kinabalu, Sabah. Its research activities center on development issues with a regional bias.) There is a basis for anticipating an improved relationship between the producers of research and its users in government circles.

EVOLUTION OF REFORMS AND STRUCTURAL ADJUSTMENT IN THE KOREAN ECONOMY

The trade and industrial policies of the Republic of Korea (henceforth referred to as Korea) have evolved with changing internal and external economic conditions. After the Korean War, Korea pursued import-substitution policies for consumer goods. Import substitution, however, was limited by the small size of the domestic market and the large amounts of capital it required.

In 1961 an outward-looking development strategy was adopted. Korea promoted exports of labor-intensive manufactured goods in which it had a comparative advantage. To promote exports, major reforms were made in industrial and trade policies. Tax, tariff, and financial incentives were provided to the export sector.

By the mid-1970s, when surplus labor from the agricultural sector disappeared and real wages began to increase, it was necessary to change the industrial structure toward capital- and technology-intensive industries. The chemical industry and heavy industries were promoted, but heavy government intervention resulted in resource misallocation, and much investment became idle.

Stabilization and liberalization policies necessary for renewed economic growth became government policy under President Chun Doo-Hwan in 1980. Since these policies demanded removal of government subsidies and protection, as well as the introduction of incomes policies, support from the general public and business community was critical to their success. Education programs to explain the background, motivation, contents, and expected results from the policy shifts were developed and introduced throughout the country.

Recently Korea has had an economic boom while maintaining price stability and balance-of-payments surplus. The new challenge is a strong demand for economic democratization in line with democratization in the political process. The Presidential Commission on Economic Restructuring was established on April 25, 1988, as an ad hoc nongovernmental advisory body to build national consensus on policies in three different fields: internationalizing the economy, restructuring industry and industrial organization, and improving social equity and the quality of life. These are the major policy directions the Korean economy must follow in the 1990s.

This chapter deals with the evolution of trade and industrial policy reforms and the structural adjustment of the Korean economy. It focuses mainly on the stabilization and liberalization policy reforms of 1980 and the policy reforms suggested by the Presidential Commission on Economic Restructuring in 1988.

The chapter starts with a historical overview of industrial and trade reforms during the three decades after the Korean War. The development of the Korean economy over the period is divided into three different stages—the period of rebuilding after the Korean War, 1953–1961; the period of export-oriented industrialization, 1962–1972; and the period of targeting heavy machinery and chemical industries, 1973–1979. There is a review of the effect of principal industrial and trade policies, with major emphasis on domestic tax policies, financial incentives, exchange-rate policies, quantitative controls, and tariff policies.

The next section of the chapter is a study of industrial and trade reforms in 1980. It analyzes the problems perceived at the time, opportunities taken to shift economic policies, policy tools adopted for the stabilization and liberalization of the economy, the decision-making process, the implementation of reforms, and the effects of policy changes.

The final section describes the 1988 Presidential Commission on Economic Restructuring. It covers the organization and major activities of the commission, major agenda for subcommittees, and summaries of the commission's report.

Industrial and Trade Policies, 1953–1979

Rebuilding after the Korean War, 1953–1961. Before the first economic development plan was launched in 1962, Korea was a traditional, closed, agrarian economy. Since the war in 1950 destroyed what little industrial base there was, Korea had to reconstruct it. The economic development policy pursued before 1962 can be loosely characterized as import substitution of nondurable consumer and intermediate goods behind a protective wall of high tariffs and stringent quotas. Soon, however, the import-substitution development strategy reached its natural limits because of its large capital requirements and the small size of the domestic market.

A significant achievement during the period was firm establishment of the foundation for human resource development. Educational facilities were expanded and enrollment in the formal education system increased rapidly at all levels. The number of college students, for example, increased from 8,000 in 1945 to 100,000 in 1960. The illiteracy rate also dropped from 78 percent to 28 percent during this period.

Export-oriented industrialization, 1962–1972. This was the period during which the Korean economy laid the foundation for continued growth based on an export-oriented industrialization strategy. Since Korea is a small economy with limited natural resources and a small domestic market, the new government adopted an outward-looking development strategy in the early 1960s. The essence of this strategy was the promotion of labor-intensive manufactured exports in which Korea had a comparative advantage. The main policy focus of the new government was extensive trade promotion coupled with heavy protection of domestic markets.

During this period, Korea carried out a major reform of industrial and trade policies. Incentives, including tax, tariff, and financial measures, were provided to export sectors.

Exemption from indirect taxes on intermediate inputs for exports, reduction of direct taxes on income earned in export activities, accelerated depreciation allowances for fixed capital used in export production, and tax exemptions on reserve funds for developing export markets and for export losses were major measures for export promotion. Imported intermediate goods and capital equipment for export production were also exempted from tariffs.

Financial incentives also played a major role in export promotion during this period. Over the past three decades, financial incentives for export promotion have taken two different forms: one is preferential allocation of financial resources to the export sector, and the other is interest-rate subsidies. In this period the government made short-term finance available for export promotion. In addition, there were export-promotion schemes that involved liberalizing credit and financial regulations, including the granting of foreign-exchange loans, offshore procurement loans guaranteed by the government, and import-export credit for overseas marketing for new export companies.

Industrial and trade policies favored export-oriented industries in general. The government exerted little effort to promote specific exports. It set annual export goals but seldom intervened in the allocation of resources for specific export industries.

In Korea imports have been primarily controlled by two policy instruments: quantitative controls and tariffs. The administration of quantitative controls and tariffs has been based on the Trade Act, the Customs Act, and various special laws. Import restrictions, through both licensing requirements and high tariffs, were widespread during this period. The degree of quantitative controls is often measured by the import- liberalization ratio—the ratio of automatically approved import items to the total number of commodity classes. When the negative list system for imports was first adopted in 1967, the ratio was 60.

To promote exports, the government corrected the overvaluation of the exchange rate in 1964. The Korean won was devalued by nearly 100 percent. Import substitution simultaneously took place in such key raw material-supplying industries as petroleum refining, fertilizers, cement, and chemical fibers. Toward the end of this period, the steel and petrochemical industries were developed.

Korea's exports grew from US$55 million in 1962 to US$1,624 million in 1972, a 40 percent real average annual growth rate. At the same time, manufactured goods, which accounted for only 27 percent of total exports in 1962, rose to 88 percent of total exports by 1972.

The 1960s was a period of substantial institutional changes. In 1962 Korea launched its First Five-Year Economic Development Plan. In line with the greater emphasis on economic planning, the Economic Planning Board was established in 1961. This organization is responsible for economic planning, national budgeting, foreign capital management, technical cooperation, and statistics administration. Functioning as a "superministry," it was the main actor in the government's intervention in the economy, orchestrating the nation's outward-looking development strategy. The Economic Planning Board not only developed short- and long-term economic plans, but was directly involved in policy implementation through its budgetary and regulatory functions.

In order to strengthen the policy planning function, various specialized policy institutes have been established since 1970 with the financial sponsorship of the government. They include the Korea Development Institute under the Economic Planning Board, Korea Institute for Industrial Economics and Technology under the Ministry of Trade and Industry, and several research institutes in science and technology.

The targeting of heavy machinery and chemical industries, 1973– 1979. The mid-1970s saw major shifts in both external and internal economic environments. Internally, in the mid-1970s, the labor surplus in the agricultural sector, which had provided cheap labor to the industrial sector, disappeared and real wages began to increase very rapidly. Therefore, Korea no longer expected to be able to maintain its comparative advantage in light manufacturing industries based on cheap labor costs. Externally, Korea was affected by two increases in petroleum prices.

In the early 1970s it was widely believed that Korea's export-oriented growth strategy, based on light manufacturing industries, would reach its limit and that Korea would lose its competitiveness with less-developed countries in those sectors. A shift toward capital- and technology- intensive industries accordingly followed.

Korea's security situation and the possible withdrawal of U.S. forces were also important reasons for undertaking this shift. The government sought to produce intermediate and capital goods in order to build a foundation for the defense industry.

The export experience of the 1960s, however, made for continuing awareness of world prices. Some of the import-substitution goods, steel for example, became competitive at international prices.

In 1973 the government announced the Heavy and Chemical Industry Development Plan. Investment did not begin until the mid-1970s because of the first increase in petroleum prices. Naphtha cracking, steel, metal products, heavy machinery, electric and electronic products, shipbuilding, and automobiles were designated as major target industries. For these industries, protection was strengthened and incentives were expanded. Unfortunately this led to an overadjustment of the industrial structure. Moreover, to achieve economies of scale in a limited domestic market, the government permitted monopolistic production in a few industries.

Incentives were provided to domestic producers in target industries in the form of preferential finance and tax exemptions or reductions. Long-term loans by public financial institutions such as the Korea Development Bank were heavily directed toward these industries, and commercial lending was strongly influenced by the government in the direction of providing finance for them. The National Investment Fund was established to provide funds at low interest rates to meet the large investment requirements of the heavy industries.

Domestic tax incentives were also provided for the target industries. They were allowed to choose one of the following three incentives: a tax credit of 8 to 10 percent of the investment amount, accelerated depreciation of up to 100 percent of the normal depreciation allowance, or exemption from corporate taxes for the first three years after the establishment of the plant and a 50 percent reduction of corporate taxes for the following two years.

During the 1970s the system of export promotion through tax measures underwent some changes. One of the major changes was brought about by the tax reform of 1977, which introduced a value-added tax in place of the previous taxes for exports. Exports continued to be exempted from indirect taxes, as a zero value-added tax rate was applied to exports in line with GATT rules.

To finance the projects of heavy and chemical industry development, however, the 50 percent reduction in corporate and income taxes on export earnings was abolished in 1973, and in 1974 a system of tariff exemption for capital equipment imported for export production was changed to an installment payment system.

Import protection had to be strengthened for the strategic industries. The government maintained high protective barriers for these targeted infant industries until they became internationally competitive. Because of renewed import protection, the import liberalization ratio declined steadily from 62 in 1968 to 51 in 1976. In the case of the broadly defined machinery industry, which included most of the target industries, the ratio declined from 56 in 1968 to 35 in 1976.

Tariff systems were reformed three times during this period: in 1973, in 1976, and in 1978. The 1973 reform was intended to restructure the tax system in such a way that tariffs on basic necessities and industrial materials were reduced while tariffs on new, heavy-industry products and luxuries were raised. The simple average of nominal tariff rates was reduced from 39 percent to 31 percent, and special tariffs were abolished. The 1976 reform did not bring about much import liberalization. Tariffs on some products were reduced but those on heavy and chemical industry products were raised. The average nominal tariff declined only from 31 percent to 30 percent. The 1978 reform resulted in the reduction of a number of very high tariffs, and the average nominal tariff was reduced to 25 percent. Liberalization was then abandoned because the balance of payments deteriorated rapidly. Unfortunately, exchange-rate policies hindered exports in the 1970s. During the period 1974–1979 the exchange rate remained unchanged, while the annual growth rate of Korea's gross national product (GNP) deflator exceeded that of the United States, its major market, by more than 10 percent. The government failed to adjust exchange rates to reflect the fall in purchasing power of the Korean currency. Overvaluation harmed export promotion and led to a subsequent devaluation of 20 percent against the U.S. dollar in 1980.

The industrialization drive toward heavy and chemical industries achieved industrial growth led by these industries, which accounted for 38 percent of the manufacturing sector's value added in 1972 and 53 percent in 1979. The share of heavy and chemical products in total exports also increased—from 21 percent in 1972 to 38 percent in 1979. The investment in these industries took place concurrently with a construction boom in the Middle East. Aggregate demand was boosted and subsequently the Korean economy overheated. It achieved a real average annual growth rate of 12 percent during the period 1976–1978.

The attempt to change the industrial structure at a stroke proved costly later. The increase in the share of heavy and chemical products in exports was accompanied by an overall slowdown in export growth. The rapid shift in the industrial structure resulted in resource misallocation. Much investment turned into idle capacity. Policies failed to develop an internationally competitive industrial sector. Consequently there was a slowdown in Korea's export-led economic growth and balance-of-payments problems. The promotion of mostly capital-intensive, heavy and chemical projects resulted in an excessive money supply. Credit was concentrated in these industries, in several large firms, while the continued development of light industries and small and medium-sized firms was relatively neglected.

Trade and Industry Reforms in 1980

Problems perceived. In 1979 the Korean economy began to suffer from rampant inflation, sluggishness in economic growth, and balance-of-payments problems. In 1979, after three years of double-digit growth, the growth rate fell to 7 percent, and the balance of payments recorded a US$4 billion deficit. The adverse effects of double-digit inflation rates spread through the economy.

The economic problems resulted from internal, as well as external, factors. The second petroleum price increase in 1979 aggravated the deterioration in the balance of payments and worsened price and wage inflation. At the same time, many economists and some technocrats believed that economic policies were also responsible for the state of the economy. There was a consensus that market principles should play a bigger role in allocating resources. It was also believed that achieving price stability was a prerequisite to renewed economic growth.

Opportunities to shift economic policies. The deterioration of the economy brought about a reshuffling of cabinet members. The deputy minister in charge of economic affairs, Mr. Shin, strongly advocated economic stabilization and liberalization policies. The late president Park endorsed the shifts in policies with some reservations since outright support would have meant the admission of mistakes in economic policies in the 1970s.

Stabilization and liberalization policies were strongly criticized by business groups who had enjoyed preferential treatment under the old system and by bureaucrats who had represented the interests of protected industrial sectors and were responsible for previous economic policies.

Nevertheless, stabilization and liberalization policies were firmly anchored with the inauguration of the Fifth Republic in 1980. The new economic policies were fully supported by President Chun's government.

Policy tools adopted. In 1980 after twenty years of successful economic growth, Korea recorded a negative growth rate of 4.8 percent and a 39 percent increase in the wholesale price index.

In pursuit of price stability, a series of tight monetary and fiscal policies were undertaken. Aggregate demand was controlled through a restrictive monetary policy aimed at limiting the overall rate of expansion of the money supply. The government also implemented a program of fiscal austerity. The concept of a zero-based budget was introduced and the national budget of 1983 was frozen at the level of the previous year. Also, agricultural subsidies were reduced from 1983 onward.

To contain inflationary expectations in wage settlements, incomes policies were pursued. By issuing suggested guidelines for wage increases and setting low schedules for salaries of government officials, the government made a strenuous effort to keep down nominal wage increases.

Korea's industrial policy also underwent a major change as a part of the liberalization effort. The government shifted its style of economic management away from the direct intervention of the 1970s toward less bureaucratic intervention, with more reliance on indirect guidance and market forces. In the 1970s targeted sectors received preferential financing and heavy protection. In the new program, all subsidized loans were eliminated, and the government no longer targeted certain areas of the economy for preferential financial treatment. This shift reflected the recognition that subsidized loan policies had resulted in overinvestment in some industries, unbalanced industrial development, and an underdeveloped financial sector.

These principles were also applied to trade policies. Changes toward a free-trade regime were introduced. Export incentives provided by financial measures were greatly reduced. The direct interest-rate subsidies were abolished, and financial subsidies in the form of preferential credit allocation declined with the reduction in preferential margins on bank credit. This reduction was attributable to monetary policy reform in 1982 and the success of price stabilization.

The most significant aspect of the trade liberalization program has been the government's import liberalization policy. To liberalize trade, the Korea Development Institute made a proposal for overall import liberalization. The proposal put a major emphasis on the elimination of quantitative restrictions, an across-the-board tariff reduction over a five-year period, and the elimination of sectoral differences in effective protection. After a series of debates, the proposal led to a liberalization program. At the end of 1983 the Ministry of Trade and Industry announced an impact liberalization program, and the Ministry of Finance announced a tariff reform plan, both covering the five-year period ending in 1988. According to the trade and industry program, the import-liberalization ratio was scheduled to rise to over 95 percent by 1988.

The tariff reform that the Ministry of Finance undertook in 1984 covered three areas: the tariff schedule, tariff rebates, and tariff administration. First, tariffs were cut on individual products by one-third over a five-year period. Second, all products, including raw materials, were required to pay some revenue tariffs. Third, tariff administration was simplified and tariff rebates phased out. Finally, an adjustment tariff was introduced to facilitate the elimination of quantitative restrictions. The government was prepared to move in the direction of trade liberalization. It was motivated by the belief that extensive import restrictions on intermediate and investment goods had an adverse impact on production efficiency, forcing domestic producers to use low-quality, high-cost domestic goods. There were also mounting pressures from industrial countries for Korea to open its domestic market.

The exchange rate was substantially devalued in early 1980 to correct the overvaluation of real effective exchange rates that had occurred previously. Since then it has floated in line with values of the currencies of Korea's major trading partners.

Liberalization of the financial sector was another key component of the economic reforms of the early 1980s. One of the first actions taken in this area was the denationalization of the five commercial banks. In addition, the barriers to entry for foreign banks were lowered, a step that is expected to increase competition and thus allocative efficiency.

Decision-making process. Until recently, policy making in Korea tended to be authoritarian, with decisions being made at the top echelons of government and little attempt made to seek consensus at the initial stage of policy making. Under Presidents Park and Chun, the National Assembly did not possess any real power, and therefore the policy-making process was virtually monopolized by the executive branch. The president was involved in all major decisions and wielded almost absolute power. Without special knowledge of economics, he was dependent on the advice and ideas of government economists and technocrats, who played decisive roles in the policy-making process.

Under President Chun many government economists assumed ministerial positions and took on the responsibilities of policy makers, further enhancing the role of government economists in the policy-making process.

In the early policy-making process, social and cultural constraints were largely ignored by government economists and technocrats. They perceived that conflicts and resistance to new policy decisions could be defused once the decisions were made. Even though groups such as the business elite, academics, and representatives of labor unions were often invited to join the policy-making process, they were formal invitations only, and the influence of these groups was quite limited. Economic policy making was authoritarian, bureaucratic, elitist, and secretive.

Implementation of policies. Full commitment to implementation is essential to the success of economic policy decisions. Stabilization and liberalization policies in 1980 were strongly supported by President Chun and carried out by a well-trained, disciplined, and motivated bureaucracy.

The Economic Planning Board played a major role at the technical level. High-level ministerial coordination was achieved through regular meetings of the Economic Minister's Council, chaired by the deputy prime minister. The periodic Economic Vice Minister's Meeting was also an effective way of strengthening coordination and communication. Communication between economic ministries was further boosted by an informal personal network of bureaucrats developed through interministerial transfer of higher civil servants.

In spite of coordination arrangements, there were tensions and conflicts over proposed new policies. The Ministry of Agriculture and Fisheries resisted the removal of agricultural subsidies and was concerned about the expected adverse impact of import liberalization on the agricultural sector. The Ministry of Trade and Industry disapproved of the speed of liberalization and the removal of subsidies to strategic industries. These conflicts were resolved, however, by the president's full commitment to policy changes.

Policy planners recognized for the first time that the success of the new economic policies required not only the strong support of the political leadership, but also the full understanding of business people, workers, farmers, and government employees. Since stabilization and liberalization policies demanded the removal of government subsidies and protection, as well as the introduction of incomes policies requiring initial sacrifices by wage earners, the support of the general public and the business community was regarded as critical to the success of the new policy reforms. To achieve this support, public information, communication, and economic education programs were developed. They explained the background, motivation, contents, and expected results from the policy shifts at all levels of private and public social organizations.

Impact of policy change. The Korean economy responded well to these economic policy reforms. With the help of a favorable external economic environment, it rebounded from the recession of 1982–1984 to the economic prosperity of 1987. The growth rate of the economy jumped to 12 percent in 1987. Korea also succeeded in curbing inflation: in the 1970s inflation averaged approximately 15 percent annually, but in 1987 wholesale prices increased by 0.3 percent and consumer prices by 3.2 percent. Price stabilization has been assisted by declines in prices of petroleum and other imported raw materials and by stabilization policies. Korea's balance of payments has also been improving rapidly. The current-account deficit, US$1.6 billion in 1983, was nearly halved to US$0.9 billion in 1985, a drop that reduced Korea's foreign borrowing requirements. The balance of payments recorded a US$9.8 billion surplus in 1987, and is expected to have a US$12 billion surplus in 1988. Following this trend, Korea moved from debtor to creditor status in 1989.

The Presidential Commission on Economic Restructuring

Recently, the internal and external environments for Korea have changed. Domestically Korea has had an economic boom while maintaining price stability and a balance-of-payments surplus. The economy has expanded and developed structurally. At the same time, political democratization has brought with it the challenge of economic democratization. Many individuals and groups are demanding a role in decision making and implementation of policies. The public is demanding a more equitable distribution of the fruits of economic growth, fair competition, and greater autonomy in labor-management relations. Externally the growing balance-of-payments surplus has brought pressure to open up domestic markets and to appreciate the Korean won.

Changes in the political environment required that the new government be more concerned about building consensus in the early stages of economic policy reforms. President Roh was elected by popular vote but failed to obtain a majority in the National Assembly. Therefore, to resolve economic problems and implement new policy reforms, it was critical that the new government policies reflect the diverse opinions and needs of the people. The Presidential Commission on Economic Restructuring was thus established to serve as a vehicle to seek national consensus.

Nature of the commission and its primary responsibilities. The commission was established on April 25, 1988, as an ad hoc nongovernmental advisory body, and it remained operative for six months. It completed its interim report and made it public at the end of August 1988; the final report was submitted to the president at the end of October 1988.

The primary responsibilities of the commission were to identify major policy issues and build national consensus on them, to make recommendations for improving social equity and the quality of life, and to make suggestions on structural adjustment and internationalization of the economy. The commission's main concern was with basic policy directions, leaving the task of formulating specific policies and programs to the government.

The commission's organization and major activities. The commission had twenty-five members appointed by the president. The members were respected civic leaders from various segments of society.

To facilitate its activities, the commission had three subcommittees: Internationalization of the Korean Economy, Industrial Restructuring, and Improving the National Standard of Living. Each subcommittee consisted of one-third of the commission members. Subcommittee meetings included nine public hearings and four open debates. All meetings of the commission and its subcommittees were open to the media. The Korea Development Institute was designated as the secretariat of the commission, to administer all procedural matters, and to prepare reports.

Report of the commission. The commission made major policy recommendations in the three different fields covered by its subcommittees.

Internationalization of the Korean economy. The commission believed that Korea still needed an outward-looking development strategy, but it pointed out that Korea should realize that this policy caused trade friction with those countries who have trade deficits with Korea. To lessen such friction Korea should reduce its current-account surplus by the early 1990s. This should be achieved through import liberalization rather than rapid appreciation of the Korean won. Domestic markets should be opened and tariffs on manufactured goods significantly reduced. The commission strongly recommended that the opening of agricultural markets should be linked to a restructuring of the agricultural industry, with producers being given sufficient notice to minimize adjustment costs. The commission also recommended opening the capital market and the service sector. It suggested that temporary adjustment assistance be provided to small and medium-sized firms. The commission emphasized international economic cooperation with both industrial and developing countries. Korea should focus on promoting friendly relations with countries along the Pacific Rim and provide more development aid.

Industrial restructuring. To sustain a high rate of economic growth in a rapidly changing international environment, Korea must continuously adjust its industrial structure toward international comparative advantage. Moreover, increases in domestic wages, continued appreciation of the won, and changes in technology require that industry re-structure. The commission recommended two general principles. First, the process of structural adjustment should be left primarily to market forces and competition. Instead of directly supporting or targeting specific industries, the government should assist in the development of science, technology, and human capital, thus creating the basic framework of the industrial structure. Second, the government should cease giving support to declining industries. Displaced workers should receive public support in the form of retraining, relocation, and other adjustment assistance needed.

For the agricultural sector the commission recommended an increase in farm size and specialization, along with greater investment of overhead capital in rural areas. It also encouraged industrial diversification in rural areas to absorb dislocated agricultural workers.

In order to promote fair competition and enhance the role of the market in allocating resources, the concentration of economic power in the hands of a few should be diffused. The commission proposed that the government strongly enforce its antimonopoly and fair-trade policies, reform the licensing and permit systems, and correct the inequitable availability of bank credits. It was suggested that the current ceiling on the total bank credit available to a conglomerate should be lowered and direct financing from the stock market should be encouraged. This would curb economic concentration and promote public ownership of large conglomerates.

The commission also pointed out that Korea's future depends upon the development of new technology and highly trained manpower. Greater efforts must therefore be made to increase the amount of research and development expenditure by providing more effective tax incentives and extending greater financial support. The commission believed that industrial technology should be developed mainly by private firms under the rules of market competition. Nevertheless, joint business-government research activities should be promoted when excessive amounts of capital, high risks, or major difficulties in internalization of success are involved.

Improving the national standard of living. The commission emphasized that the government should take steps to improve social equity and the quality of life. Korea's high-growth policy did not benefit all people equally, and the welfare of some sectors and groups lagged behind that of the nation as a whole. Therefore tax reforms and government spending to give greater priority to lower-income groups were advised. The commission also argued in favor of expanding vocational training and work-related education programs, in order to improve the economic self-sufficiency of the poor.

The commission noted that regional imbalance was one factor responsible for social inequality. To promote regionally balanced growth, increased social overhead capital investment and public services to neglected regions were recommended.

The commission also emphasized that the social security system and low-income housing should be expanded to better assist those in need. Finally, the commission urged that appropriate measures be taken to encourage the establishment of cooperative and autonomous labor-management relations. It advocated that labor union activities be guaranteed. Smooth labor-management relations were seen to be crucial for the future development of the Korean economy.

TRADE AND INDUSTRY REFORMS AND POLICY RESEARCH IN CHINA

Since the late 1970s, with the process of economic reform in China, there has been a significant change in the structure of consumption and large increases in imports of consumer goods. New industries developed to meet domestic demand, but they relied heavily on imported equipment and materials. Balance-of-trade problems emerged, as China's traditional exports of primary products could not keep pace with the increased demand for imports. By the mid-1980s the trade deficit was close to US$15 billion.

New industries tended to be too diversified, small scale, and inefficient. In China production capacity expands on the basis of bureaucratic decisions, with few market mechanisms operating. The resulting industrial structure is capital intensive and makes minimal use of local inputs.

In addition, the central government controls a large share of the foreign-exchange earnings accruing to local governments, and this reduces the incentive for local governments to expand industry in the most efficient manner.

Finally, highly centralized planning has resulted in a dual economic structure in China, with the agricultural sector lagging behind the industrial sector.

The author is particularly indebted to Mr. Zhang Shaojie, Ms. Diao Xinshen, and Dr. Cao Yuanzheng, whose experience and comments contributed to the writing of this chapter.

At the start of 1988 the Chinese government began a strategy for coastal economic development. This placed great importance on attracting foreign investment, developing labor intensive industries, increasing exports, and allowing local governments and enterprises more freedom in foreign trade.

Prior to 1979 there were few professional policy researchers within the Chinese government and no institutional arrangements to assist policy makers. Once the need for reform of the economy was recognized, however, the role of policy research was also seen to be important. There are now a number of government research agencies doing policy studies. There are mechanisms for meetings and coordination between government departments and these agencies. In addition there are some private and company financed research institutions, as well as individuals from universities, international organizations, and abroad, who are able to play a role in policy research.

Compared with other countries, however, policy research in China is still in its infancy. Researchers are often discouraged by the lack of institutional arrangements to guarantee them a role in policy making, they are restricted by the poor availability of data, and many lack the training and education they require.

Economic Reforms and the Demand for Imports

Since the start of the economic reform and the opening to the outside world, domestic demand has increased greatly and the structure of demand has become more and more dependent on the world market.

Changes in consumption and the increase in imports. As China began its economic reform and opened up to the outside world, personal incomes rose and consumption increased. China's industry possessed the potential to increase production, especially in the industries producing traditional consumer goods such as cloth, matches, soap, bicycles, watches, sewing machines, and so on. Industry's response to the increase in demand was at first adequate, but the structure of consumption soon changed. Consumption in the outside world became an example that Chinese consumers wanted to follow, and spending on durable consumer goods increased at a much higher rate than income. Between 1981 and 1987, while urban per capita income increased by only about 40 percent, the purchase of washing machines, refrigerators, and color television sets increased dramatically. Refrigerator purchases increased ninetyfold. In most countries black-and-white television appears before color television, but in China the black-and-white period was scarcely present. Color television purchases increased fifty-ninefold between 1981 and 1987.

TABLE 5.1   Value and Growth of Foreign Trade, 1979–1987

	Exports		Imports		
	Value (US$ billion)	Annual growth rate (percent)	Value (US$ billion)	Annual growth rate (percent)	Trade balance (US$ billion)
1979	13.66	40.1	15.67	43.9	−2.01
1980	18.27	33.7	19.55	24.8	−1.28
1981	22.01	20.5	22.01	12.6	0.00
1982	22.32	1.4	19.28	−12.4	3.04
1983	22.23	−0.4	21.39	10.9	0.84
1984	26.14	17.6	27.41	28.1	−1.27
1985	27.35	4.6	42.25	54.1	−14.90
1986	30.94	13.1	42.91	1.6	−11.97
1987	39.44	27.5	43.21	0.7	−3.77

SOURCE: *Statistical Yearbook of China*, 1988.

Consumption by institutions also broadened. As such consumption was less restricted by income and price, its rate of increase and range surpassed those of consumption by individuals. This further intensified the growth of China's consumption. Between 1981 and 1985 institutional spending on imported products increased eighteenfold for air conditioners, twelvefold for photocopiers, fourfold for video cassette players, thirty-sevenfold for floor polishers, ninefold for cars, and thirty-onefold for other office supplies (Diao et al. 1988, 14).

These drastic changes in consumption helped introduce a market-oriented economy and upgrade the industrial structure. On the other hand, the sudden change in the structure of consumption, together with the scale of demand, went far beyond China's existing industrial production capacity. As a result, China greatly increased imports of consumer goods. The rise in imports started in the early 1980s and peaked in 1984 and 1985 (see Table 5.1).

New consumer-goods industries and their dependence on imports. The changes in demand for consumer products promoted the rise of new consumer goods industries, which in turn increased reliance on imports. China has become one of the world's top two producers of television sets and washing machines. As in most developing countries, production first took the form of assembly lines utilizing imported raw materials, components, and machinery. In 1985 China produced 17 million television sets, but only 8 million, or less than half, of the tubes, were produced domestically. To produce 1.4 million refrigerators, China spent US$130 million on importing parts, about US$93 for every refrigerator produced.

Many new industries, including consumer durables, require steel sheets, imports of which account for more than 40 percent of the total requirements. China's newly developed consumer products industries, though supported to a great extent by imports, are motivated by domestic demand. Their production is domestically oriented, and there is little motivation to export because the structure of tariff and nontariff protection ensures high profits in production for domestic markets and creates a bias against production for export. Dependence on imports has to be supported by the export of traditional products, especially primary products. But traditional exports cannot equal the new industries' rapidly growing demand for imports. The overvaluation of the yuan creates a bias against all exports. The result is an unfavorable balance of payments.

Inefficient introduction of new technology. China's huge domestic market should provide a good basis for the establishment of modern industry, but this advantage is not being utilized. New consumer goods production is excessively diversified, small scale, and hence, inefficient.

China began producing washing machines in 1978. The number of factories reached 300, but fell to 130 in 1984. In 1985 there were still over eighty factories with an annual production capacity of 10,000 or more. Among these, however, only fourteen factories reached minimum economies of scale, that is, had an annual capacity of 200,000 units. In Japan by contrast, 5.28 million washing machines were produced by only fifteen manufacturers in 1984.

In 1985 there were more than one hundred television manufacturers in China. The Republic of Korea on the other hand, produces more than 10 million television sets a year in only six factories, and three of these factories turn out 93 percent of the color sets and 75 percent of the black-and-white sets.

In 1985 China produced only 87,000 mini automobiles in thirteen assembly plants; only 30 percent of the content was domestic.

Production capacity has been created mainly by importing assembly lines and key equipment. The expenditure of foreign exchange on a large number of small-scale and diverse factories not only lowered the efficiency of foreign-exchange use, but also sacrificed economies of scale and hampered the process of digesting new technology and replacing imported parts, materials, and related products. It also resulted in surplus production capacity. The production of refrigerators is an example. The total output was 4 million units in 1987, but production capacity of the forty-one factories licensed by the Ministry of Light Industry is 11.3 million units. Such a large production capacity, even in the absence of further expansion of production and imports, would exceed domestic demand. Meanwhile, all production is dependent on imports of parts, thus putting enormous pressure on the balance of payments.

In a market economy the emergence of many small enterprises as new industries develop is not a problem provided that protection—either through tariffs, import licenses, or production licenses—does not hamper the process of competition. Economic scales of production can then be achieved, and a division of production will emerge among large and small enterprises. In China, however, production capacity does not expand in line with the market, but according to bureaucratic design. There is no provision for firms to exit through elimination or merger. It is nearly impossible for enterprises to go bankrupt and difficult to merge enterprises that belong to different bureaucratic administrations. The structure of protection and the unduly low price of capital encourages enterprises to engage in assembling final products with few bearing the risk of making the parts.

China's incentive structure also encourages relatively high capital intensity and hence discourages employment. It promotes an inappropriate use of high technology and minimal use of local inputs.

Problems in the Foreign-Trade System

Before 1978 China's foreign trade was highly centralized and planned. There was no access to world markets, partly the result of an outside blockade, and there was a heavy emphasis on self-reliance for fear of falling into others' control. Foreign trade was monopolized by the state. Since domestic prices were fixed and prices on the world market fluctuated, the central government did all the purchasing and selling and was wholly responsible for the ensuing gains and losses. This resulted in the separation of producers from the world market, with the former unable to show concern for the characteristics and changes in demand.

Foreign trade has been changed drastically since 1979. As a result of the decentralization of foreign-trade management, many local governments and enterprises obtained foreign-trade rights. They were encouraged to raise their production for export, and exports were promoted. Until 1984 China was able to export more than it imported. The export structure improved along the lines of comparative advantage, with exports of industrial products growing more rapidly than exports of primary products.

After 1984, as domestic demand for raw materials and primary products grew, imports of raw materials rose dramatically. Between 1980 and 1985, imports of steel products cost US$6.3 billion, an amount equal to 15 percent of total export revenue. The rapid increase in imports resulted in a decline in foreign-exchange reserves, an increase in foreign debt, and foreign-trade deficits. It is commonly thought that imports of consumer goods were responsible for the increase in imports, but the growing demand for industrial inputs was the main culprit.

In order to promote exports local governments are allowed to retain a portion of the foreign exchange they have earned. In 1985 the central government took 60 percent of foreign exchange, leaving 40 percent to local administrations. In 1986 the share was 50 percent each; in 1987 it became 40 percent central and 60 percent local. The retained portion does not consist of foreign exchange, but of quotas. Local governments use these quotas in three ways:

- To develop local industries. These are mainly manufacturing industries, but because of the incentive system they are mostly assembly industries with all the problems outlined above.

- To import consumer goods. These they can sell profitably in the domestic market.

- To pay local debts.

Local governments spend most of their foreign exchange on the first item. They do not plan for the recurring foreign-exchange requirements of their manufacturing plants, and depend on the central government to meet these requirements. This again forces the central government to spend foreign exchange, even local quotas, on importing raw materials.

Problems in Industrial Structure and Distribution

Contrary to the quick reaction of consumer-goods industries toward increased demand, the response of China's basic and intermediate industries to the demands of the consumer-goods industries has been extremely slow. China has imported many refrigerator assembly lines, but China's electrical equipment industry cannot supply the compressors and PTC relays, so these must be imported. Imports, therefore, lead to further imports.

Historically the western and central parts of China provided natural resources and the eastern coastal parts were manufacturing centers. Since the start of economic reform, the decentralization of finance, and the expansion of enterprise management rights, a new trend has

TABLE 5.2   Growth of Rural Industries, 1981–1987

Year	Number of enterprises (million)	Number of workers (million)	Total income (US$ billion)
1981	1.34	29.70	67.04
1982	1.36	31.13	77.18
1983	1.35	32.35	92.87
1984	1.65	38.48	126.82
1985	1.57	41.52	182.74
1986	1.52	43.92	222.36
1987	1.58	47.02	293.41

SOURCE: *Statistical Yearbook of China.*

emerged in which the central and western provinces, driven by local interests and the national incentive system, have started to develop their own manufacturing industries.

This change, of course, played an important role in helping develop those provinces. At the same time, it increased competition for resources and markets. The old industrial provinces became short of raw material supplies and had to let their production capacity lay idle, while the new industrial areas found it extremely hard to compete in the market. As a result, regional protection was introduced. This reduces the general efficiency of resource allocation and erodes the economic benefits brought about by reform.

China's industrialization was carried out by highly centralized planning, which led to a dual economic structure consisting of a relatively developed industrial sector and a backward agricultural sector. China's economic reform first started in the weak agricultural sector. As agriculture developed, reform shifted to rural industries. Total income produced by rural industries grew from US$67 billion in 1981 to US$293 billion in 1987 (see Table 5.2).

The development of rural and urban industries led to a rapid growth in the demand for capital, raw materials, energy, and technology, but the system of planning and incentives could not create an appropriate response in basic and intermediate industries, and as a result, prices rose.

Changing Strategies

To address these problems in China's economic development there have been a number of development strategies related to trade and industry. In 1980 special economic zones in Guangdong and Fujian were set up, and later a number of open cities and areas were established as windows to introduce foreign investment and technology. At about the same time, some economists put forward the "strategic shift for development," which basically proposed to shift the emphasis from heavy industry to light industry and to achieve development mostly by technology advancement.

In 1982 coastal cities were encouraged to use the world market, foreign investment, and technology to speed up their development, which would then spread to the inland economy. Foreign investment and technology were introduced to a limited extent.

In 1983 the theory of "gradual development" proposed that eastern China be developed first, with development moving gradually westward to inland areas. In 1984 some economists countered this with a theory of "antigradual development," which suggested that inland areas could develop faster by introducing advanced technology directly.

In 1987 the theory of "grand international circulation" proposed that China's development and modernization required it to join the international economy. The government began a strategy for coastal economic development in the beginning of 1988. The strategy aims to

- attract more foreign investment by making use of the coastal areas' advantages of abundant unskilled labor, some commercial expertise, and some transport facilities and infrastructure

- develop labor-intensive industries and industries that process imported materials, and launch more foreign-funded enterprises, joint ventures, and coproduction enterprises using foreign investment

- have enterprises in coastal areas enter the world market in order to develop the local economy as well as other parts of China

- reform the traditional foreign-trade management system to allow local governments and enterprises a greater role in foreign trade

- encourage rural enterprises in coastal areas to be more competition conscious and more export oriented in order to increase their foreign-exchange earnings

- improve enterprise management by introducing the contract system and inviting foreign entrepreneurs into direct management of joint ventures and coproduction enterprises

This approach to China's reform and development has strategic significance. The strategy is not to deal with the problems by looking at issues individually. It also considers the problem of China's economic reform as well as economic development. Many problems arose during the process of economic reform, including imports of consumer luxuries, excessive imports of raw materials, excessive reliance on imports and the world market, the character of the foreign-trade system, and so on. If dealt with on their own, the solutions suggested might be suppression of consumption, more control of investment, and recentralization of foreign trade. Such measures might help for a while, but in the long run they would harm China's economic reform and development. The strategy selected, by contrast, stresses that the development of an export-oriented economy in the coastal areas requires the acceleration of reform in the foreign-trade system and further stimulus to enterprise.

The strategy proposes to use the world market to upgrade the industrial structure and deal with China's shortage of capital. It places great importance on exporting. The strategy also requires the coastal areas to develop outwardly—to leave the domestic market and resources to the inland areas.

By making use of China's abundant labor force to develop exports of labor intensive products, the strategy points to a realistic approach for China's industrialization. Surplus rural labor will be able to shift to industry, thus meeting the need of China's rural areas for industrialization. The foreign exchange earned through this strategy can be used to provide capital and technology for heavy and intermediate industries in order to modernize urban industries. Accumulation as a result of industrialization will increase the demand for and supply of agricultural output. In this way, an economic structure with tight internal connections will evolve.

Policy Research in China

The only policy research bodies that existed in China before 1979 were within the government. These included the State Council's Office for Policy Investigation and Study, the Central Planning Committee's Office for Policy Study, and the offices for policy study in various ministries. These offices were not really policy research institutions. They were government agencies that served their leaders by gathering information and occasionally doing policy analysis and providing recommendations. Few of their staff were professionally trained policy researchers. In addition there were no institutional arrangements such as presidential advisers or advisory committees in the Chinese government to assist policy makers.

After 1979, however, as China started to reform its economy, the government began to realize the importance of policy study, and the demand for policy research increased. As a result, new policy research organizations have emerged and the role of policy-study bodies within government agencies has changed. National policy-research institutions such as the State Council's Research Center for Social and Technological Development, the State Council's Research Center for Rural Development, and the State Commission for Restructuring the Economic System were founded. The first two are ministerial level policy-research agencies, while the third is both a policy-implementing ministry and a research organization for reform policies. Unlike earlier offices for policy study, these policy-research institutions are more open and many of their staff members are professional.

The role of policy-research bodies within government agencies has changed. They serve their department leaders only in a narrow sense; in order to improve policy making and implementation they have strengthened their policy study. Some have their own graduate programs (the Financial Research Institute of the People's Bank of China and the Research Institute of the State Planning Commission).

Coordination between different government departments and agencies has been improved with the setting up of special committees and regular meetings. The reform of foreign-trade policy, for instance, involves not only the Ministry of Foreign Economic Relations and Trade, but also the Ministry of Finance, the State Planning Commission, the People's Bank of China, the State Commission for Machinery Building, and others.

A number of special policy-research institutions have emerged. At the government level they include, for example, the Economic System Reform Institute of China and the Institute for Rural Development. These institutes are usually closely connected with the government. The former is affiliated with the State Commission for Restructuring the Economy and the latter with the State Council's Research Center for Rural Development. Private institutions include the Asian Research Institute in Shanghai, the Development Institute of Southeast Chemical College, and the Beijing Economics Institute. These are small institutes with few and mostly part-time staff. Since they have to raise their own funds, they generally contract for specific policy study areas.

In order to serve their own interests and influence policy making, large companies have started to set up policy research institutions. These include the Institute for Strategic Studies of Kanghua Company, the CITIC Research International of China International Trust and Investment Corporation, and the Center for Development Studies of the Capital Iron and Steel Company. Apart from these organizations, research institutes of the Chinese Academy of Social Sciences and the

Chinese Academy of Sciences, individual researchers at universities, international organizations, and foreign scholars are all playing an increasingly important role in China's public policy making.

Channels of communication. There are five ways for policy researchers to communicate with policy makers: first, through commissioned reports or internal government references and memoranda; second, by oral reports and internal government meetings; third, through conferences and symposia; fourth, in published books and papers; and fifth, through the mass media. Among these the first two are most effective and play the most important role in communicating policy information. Policy makers depend on government researchers or researchers having close association with government agencies for policy information and consultation. Conferences and public discussions of policy issues are popular channels of communication, but they do not have as important a role as government research. Published books and papers tend to be out of date because of the time needed for publication and are rarely read by policy makers. They are, however, widely used by researchers. Newspapers and periodicals, but especially newspapers, have a role second only to internal government channels. Newspaper articles are more likely to be read by policy makers than books or learned papers. Television and radio are least effective because they are controlled by the government and used to educate the public in order to facilitate policy implementation, rather than influence decision making.

The Role of Policy Research in Trade and Industry Reform

Policy research has played an increasingly important role in trade and industry reform since 1979. On the one hand, policy makers are becoming increasingly aware of the importance of policy research and are more willing to listen to researchers; on the other hand, researchers are more interested in policy research and eager to influence policy making. Compared with other countries, however, policy research in China is still limited.

In general it has been easier to identify problems than to provide feasible policy recommendations. While policy makers have to take account of political realities, policy researchers often do not. Policy researchers also adopt a long-term approach while policy makers are more concerned with the short term. These differences can form obstacles to communication and cooperation, and may even alienate policy researchers from policy makers.

The lack of institutional arrangements to guarantee policy research a legitimate role in policy making also limits its role. Policy studies or consultations take place only when policy makers decide that they are necessary. As a result researchers are often discouraged.

Another method often adopted by policy researchers is to package the policy information to suit the needs of policy makers. Perhaps out of necessity, Chinese policy researchers are quite good at this packaging, and many reform policy recommendations have been adopted because of their good packages. An outstanding example of good packaging is enterprise sharing, first proposed in 1985. The argument was then focused on the government's role as shareholder, and the issue was too remote and too academic to be an attractive policy option. In 1988 and 1989, however, sharing has drawn much attention and is now being adopted as one of the major schemes in enterprise reform. It is being adopted because sharing, a typical way of privatization, has been packaged as an anti-inflation policy. A number of other privatization schemes, such as commercialization of housing, selling of small enterprises, and so forth, have all been proposed and adopted as policies to deal with inflation, which has become the biggest headache for policy makers.

Another factor that hampers the role of policy research is the availability of data. While the situation has improved in the past few years, some data is still not available to nongovernment researchers, who must obtain it from World Bank reports. There are only general annual figures of some monetary items; producer goods price indexes and import and export price indexes are not available. So it is difficult to assess and analyze the trade situation.

The educational qualifications of Chinese policy researchers is also a problem, especially because of the interruption to education in the late 1960s and early 1970s. Many researchers lack systematic training in economics or other disciplines. Nevertheless, training of researchers is being emphasized, and more people are being sent to study abroad.

Conclusion

To enhance the importance of policy research in public decision making, much effort must be made to

- further open the public decision making process and institutionalize the role of policy research

- improve communication and understanding between policy researchers and decision makers, perhaps through mobility between the two groups

- develop the information system, release data currently classified as confidential, and make more data available

- improve the academic qualifications of policy researchers by providing opportunities to study and work abroad and participate in research projects with researchers from other countries

- educate the policy makers to appreciate the importance of policy research and consultation

TRADE AND INDUSTRY REFORMS
IN THE PHILIPPINES, 1980–1987

Meaningful reforms in trade and industry are usually the result of a drawn out process, in which there are short-run winners and short-run losers. The more comprehensive the reforms, the more potential losers there are, and the more harsh and drawn out is the tug-of-war. Many times the reform initiatives succeed in producing only cosmetic changes. Advocates of change normally swim against the dominant coalitional current, and some economic cataclysm is usually required to turn the tide in favor of the reformers. The conservative epithet, "If it ain't broke, don't fix it," usually prevails. The reason for this is that while the benefits of reform are usually a few years down the road, the costs are immediate. The losers are acutely aware of the costs, but any benefits for the winners are largely notional. What's more, the winners may themselves be notional. As Planning Secretary Solita Monsod publicly rues, "Unfortunately, 90 percent of my constituency is still unborn."

This chapter deals with trade and industry reforms of the Philippine industrial restructuring program since 1980 and examines what role economic policy research played in the process. Two books, one written by John Power and Gerardo Sicat (1971) and the second a collection of papers on trade and industrial policy done by several authors under the leadership of Romeo Bautista and John Power (1979), were particularly influential. The latter book was also used by the political leadership to quiet whatever little dissent was left in the ranks of businessmen and gave the academic technocrats a stronger basis.

After 1983, the series of crisis monographs from the University of the Philippines School of Economics may have been decisive in salvaging some of the reforms under the new government. These monographs were decidedly promarket where the crisis rhetoric was antimarket and antireform. This series of monographs became the basis of the new government's public agenda.

The first section of this article details the major trade and industrial policy reforms from 1980 to 1987. The second discusses the major coalitions that played a part in the commitment phase of the structural adjustment loan and its related reforms. The third section of the chapter describes the decision-making processes under the current government, including the role of the series of crisis monographs from the School of Economics. Finally, the production of policy studies is discussed.

Historical Background

Balance-of-payments crises occur frequently in the Philippine economy. There was one in 1949, another in early 1960, still another in 1970, and a somewhat delayed one in 1983. At the core, balance-of-payments crises indicate that a nation is spending more than it earns. One way to do this is by excessive borrowing domestically, which leads to inflation, exchange-rate pressures, and a possible balance-of-payments crisis if the borrowing is used unproductively. Another is by borrowing from abroad. If the foreign borrowing is used unproductively the debt service may cause a crisis. A third route is a drastic drop in the terms of trade due to falling export prices or rising import prices. A fourth is a temporary massive inflow of foreign savings, which induces inflation and persistently higher import spending. In each of these cases, the failure of the exchange rate to adjust quickly is central in precipitating the crisis.

The crisis of 1949 resulted from a slow pressure buildup due to very high government election spending and an inflow of foreign savings (war damage claims). The exchange rate did not budge in 1949 and throughout the 1950s. There was a slow buildup of pressure from imported inputs, which exploded in 1960. Massive government spending in the late 1960s precipitated the crisis of 1970. Heavy foreign borrowing used unproductively forced a crisis of debt service in 1983. This cycle of deficit growth financing and balance-of-payments crisis puts the Philippines in the mold of the Latin American economy. The challenge in the long run is to break the cycle.

Trade and Industry Reforms

The industrial restructuring program that began in 1980 is the most comprehensive and ambitious in Philippine history.

The tariff reform program. The tariff reform program started in 1981 with the objective of establishing more uniform tariff levels. It was largely completed in 1985 (Medalla and Power 1986). Its main features were

- reduction of peak nominal rates on nonessential consumer and unclassified consumer goods from 100 percent to 50 percent

- raising the minimum tariff from 0 to 10 percent

- reduction of the number of categories of tariff levels from fourteen to ten

- reduction of the average tariff on manufactured goods from 42.38 percent to 28.06 percent, and reduction of the average tariff for agricultural goods from 56.38 percent to 33.08 percent

Table 6.1 gives the distribution of tariff lines by nominal rate. Note the bunching of lines between 10 percent and 50 percent in 1985. Table 6.2 gives the average statutory rates for different input-output table sectors. Note the drop from 56 percent to 33 percent for agriculture and a drop from 42 percent to 28 percent for manufacturing. Table 6.3 gives the average effective protection rates for major commodity groupings.

Indirect taxes. Indirect taxes had protective effects because of the following:

- Nominal tax rates on semi-essential and nonessential imports were higher than those on domestically produced counterparts.

- Advance sales tax and compensating tax on imports were payable upon release from customs while local sales taxes were payable within twenty days after each quarter.

- The tax base was raised by a markup system of 25 percent for essential, 50 percent for semi-essential, and 100 percent for nonessential goods.

TABLE 6.1   Distribution of Tariffs by Nominal Rate

Tariff levels	1981 Number of tariff lines	1981 Percent of total	1985 Number of tariff lines	1985 Percent of total
Specific	2	0.14	2	0.14
Free	3	0.21	3	0.21
5 percent	14	0.99	14	0.99
10 percent	380	27.00	334	23.80
20 percent	282	20.00	335	23.88
30 percent	194	14.00	284	20.24
40 percent	87	6.00	100	7.13
50 percent	151	11.00	331	23.59
60 percent	59	4.20	0	0
70 percent	139	9.90	0	0
75 percent	2	0.14	0	0
80 percent	58	4.10	0	0
90 percent	29	2.00	0	0
100 percent	2	0.14	0	0
Total tariff lines	1,402		1,403	
Total tariff levels	14		8	

SOURCE: Medalla and Power 1986.

TABLE 6.2   Average Statutory Tariff Rates (percentage)

Input-output sector	Industry/industry group	1979	1985
01–14	Agriculture, fishery and forestry	56.38	33.08
01–02	Palay	70.00	50.00
03	Corn	70.00	50.00
04	Coconut, including copra	85.00	35.00
05	Sugarcane	70.00	50.00
06	Banana	100.00	50.00
07	Other crops	27.18	13.05
08–09	Livestock	53.57	26.47
10–11	Poultry	74.28	47.78
12–13	Fishery	93.75	33.08
14	Forestry	46.00	27.22
15–21	Mining and quarrying	16.38	13.09
15	Copper mining	10.00	10.00
16	Gold and silver ore mining	10.00	10.00
17	Chromium ore mining	10.00	10.00
18	Nickel mining	10.00	10.00
19	Other metal mining	10.00	10.00

(continued on next page)

TABLE 6.2 (continued)

Input-output sector	Industry/industry group	1979	1985
20	Salt mining	30.00	15.00
21	Other nonmetallic mining/quarrying	18.12	14.70
22–58	Manufacturing	42.38	28.06
22–30	Food manufactures	60.00	33.68
31	Beverage industries	78.46	50.00
32	Tobacco manufactures	65.00	42.30
33	Textile manufactures	53.53	35.44
34	Footwear and wearing apparel	85.62	48.86
35–36	Wood and cork products	53.42	32.32
37	Furniture and fixtures	82.00	45.00
38	Paper and paper products	55.71	30.70
39	Publishing and printing	56.25	24.16
40	Leather and leather products	69.00	30.00
41	Rubber and plastic products	37.43	26.35
42–45	Chemicals and chemical products	23.39	17.53
46–50	Products of petroleum and coal	20.55	17.50
51–52	Nonmetallic mineral products	47.30	34.54
53	Basic metal products	21.20	16.13
54	Metal industries	44.75	35.24
55	Machinery except electrical	24.32	22.15
56	Electrical machinery	38.05	27.55
57	Transport equipment	26.00	23.66
58	Miscellaneous manufactures	46.66	30.85

SOURCE: Medalla and Power 1986.

TABLE 6.3   Average Effective Rates of Protection (percentage)

	1979	1985
All sectors	24	12
Exportables	–3	–3
Importables	44	25
Primary and agriculture	1	–1
Manufacturing	40	23
Exportables	1	1
Importables	58	33

SOURCE: Medalla and Power 1986.

As much as one-third of effective protection to manufacturing resulted from indirect taxes. The current sales tax rates are now equal for both imported and domestically produced goods and the markup system was abolished.

TABLE 6.4   Number of Items Regulated, Banned, and Liberalized, 1980–1986

Year	Regulated		Number of PSCC lines banned	Number of PSCC lines liberalized
	Number of PSCC lines	Cumulative		
1980	6	549	1301	0
1981	20	557	1038	263
1982	312	869	428	610
1983	585	1451	380	48
1984	45	1496	380	0
1985	0	1470	334	72
1986	0	675	193	936

SOURCE: IBRD 1987.

Import liberalization program. Perhaps more important than the tariff reform program is the import liberalization program. Table 6.4 gives the number of Philippine Standard Commodity Classification (PSCC) lines regulated, banned, and liberalized from 1980 to 1986. The cumulative number of items regulated is also shown. The liberalized group, nonexistent in 1980, had 936 items in 1986. The process, however, stumbled in 1984 when the sum of regulated and banned items totaled 1,876 compared with 1,850 in 1980. Import liberalization was officially suspended at the end of 1984, in response to the balance-of-payments crisis, and other import restrictions were introduced including foreign-exchange rationing and a no dollar imports scheme.

Industrial policy reforms. The new initiatives in industrial policy were embodied in a new law, *Batasang Pambamso* 391 of 1983, which supplanted an earlier law, Presidential Decree 1781. The latter had employed the concept of "measured capacity" to either extend or withhold incentives. Measured capacity determined whether an industry was overcrowded, in which case further entrants were denied incentives. This restricted entry and fostered inefficiency among existing firms. The incentives also tended to favor capital use. Incentives were based on investment rather than value-added or efficiency criteria. Because of this, the incentives tended to emphasize a domestic, instead of outward, orientation. The 1983 law improved on the earlier one in these areas. It simplified incentives, cutting their number from fourteen to eight, and the emphasis on the use of measured capacity was reduced. Value added became the basis for incentives in the form of tax credits. Capital incentives were reduced from between 31 percent and 64 percent to between 7 percent and 24 percent. Table 6.5 summarizes the fiscal incentives as of 1986. Export projects were given much more emphasis, although the accession of the Philippines to the General Agreement on Tariffs and Trade

TABLE 6.5   Summary of the Board of Investment Fiscal Incentives, 1986

Incentives	Rate (%) or eligibility		Conditions
	Pioneer	Nonpioneer	
Tax credit on net value earned[a]	10	5	Available only for new or expanded capacity. Tax credit earned for the first five years of commercial production.
Tax credit on net local content of exports[b]	10	10	Available for years in full operation, and additional five years based on increment for local content.
			For existing producers tax credit payable on increment of local content only.[c]
Tax credit for taxes and duties paid on raw material supplies used in export production	Yes	Yes	Available for an indefinite period to all export producers.
Exemption from export taxes and fees	Yes	Yes	Available for an indefinite period to all export producers.
Exemption from taxes and duties on imported capital equipment	100	50	Available for an indefinite period to all export producers. Recovered by reducing future tax credit on net value earned and net local content.
Tax credit for locally purchased capital equipment (equal to value of taxes and duties that would be waived for imported equipment)	100	50	As above.
Net operating loss carry-over	Yes	Yes	Losses incurred in any of the first ten years of operations may be carried over as a deduction from taxable income for a maximum period of six years following the period in which the loss was incurred.
Tax credit for withholding tax on interest on foreign loans	Yes	No	Available for loans taken during the first five years of registration or operation.

NOTE: Based on Presidential Decree 1789, as amended by *Batasang Pambamso* 391 Executive Order 1945.

a. Net value earned is calculated as value of sales minus purchase of raw materials, supplies, utilities and some specifically excluded commodities.

b. Net local content is calculated as value of sales minus imported raw materials and supplies, depreciation of capital equipment and some specifically excluded commodities. To be phased out by 1990 under Executive Order 1045.

c. Registered enterprises already engaged at the time of registration in production, manufacture of processing.

SOURCE: IBRD 1987.

(GATT) made certain export incentives unacceptable (tariff and tax exemptions on imports of machinery have to be repaid, and tax credits equal to 20 percent of export sales have to be given up).

Financial sector reforms, 1981–1983. Interest-rate ceilings were lifted, and the concept of universal banking was introduced. Banks were encouraged to merge and provide services once provided separately by specialized institutions—these included normal credit operations, equity investment, underwriting securities, and long-term credit extension. Preferential and targeted credit programs administered by government financial institutions were discontinued as the institutions were restructured.

Exchange rate. The peso was floated, but the central bank continued to support it through foreign-exchange dealings, unofficial approval and management of the infamous "Binondo Central Bank" (where a few dollar traders were given the unofficial monopoly), and the use of central bank Certificate of Indebtedness and government securities. Thus, movement of exchange rates within a very narrow allowable band resulted in substantial overvaluation of the peso. In the period 1984–1985, for example, the governor of the central bank, Jose B. Fernandez, drastically raised Certificate of Indebtedness to ease the pressure on the exchange rate brought about by massive spending during the June 1984 parliamentary elections. Some firms had to stop operations due to the very high cost of money, but the black market rate fell from P26 to P18 to the dollar as a result.

Agriculture. In 1985 the government lifted price controls on milled rice and deregulated the fertilizer trade. Imports of fertilizer were allowed to traders other than the local fertilizer manufacturing cartel. Urea- and potassium-based ingredients were exempted from duties and advance sales tax. Direct imports of nitrogen and potassium ingredients were allowed, but with a 20 percent duty and a 10 percent advance sales tax on phosphate imports.

Reforms under the Aquino government. In December 1986 a new medium-term development plan was adopted for an agriculture-based, employment-oriented recovery strategy. It displayed a strong market orientation and adopted respect for human rights, social justice, greater efficiency, and minimal government intervention as guiding principles. The plan closely followed the "agenda for reform" released in May 1986.

- *Import liberalization.* An additional one thousand import items were liberalized and tariff exemptions lifted. Only 673 items remain in the regulated list, and future liberalization is being considered.

- *Agricultural market liberalization.* Sugar and coconut monopolies were dismantled. Export taxes on all agricultural products except logs were abolished; government monopolies over wheat, flour, and feed imports were abolished; the export ban on copra was lifted; selective credit policies and subsidies were abolished; and the central bank rediscount rate became market-aligned.

- *Privatization.* The Cabinet Committee on Privatization oversees the overall privatization effort being implemented by the Asset Privatization Trust. The government has approved the privatization of eighty-six public corporations, with a total book value of US$1.8 billion. The plan is to privatize assets totaling about US$20 billion in book value. More than US$20 million worth of assets were either sold or allowed to be bought out. Decisions on the larger, more profitable corporations, however, have been deferred. Conflicts of interest connected with government agents heading privatizable corporations have surfaced. In some cases economic issues are involved. For example, the privatization of the Philippine National Oil Corporation may not be pursued because it is seen as a tool against petroleum transnationals; the Philippine National Bank in theory keeps the banking cartel in check. Valuation of assets, as well as legal problems, is also bogging down the process. On the other hand, as privatization income is earmarked for land reform, the pressure for privatization may remain strong.

- *Industrial promotion.* The 1987 Omnibus Investment Code seems to incorporate features that militate against efficiency: incentives are once again based on investment rather than performance, measured capacity has resurfaced as a criterion, and capital bias is back. There is an attempt to revive the car manufacturing program. Incentives to small firms are lacking. Overall, the 1987 regulations may be a step back.

- *Exchange rate.* Although some movement is observed in the exchange rate, the central bank is administering the rate within a narrow band.

The Aquino government thus carried out the bulk of the reforms involving import liberalization and agricultural market liberalization. The privatization program continues at a slow pace. But there are calls for price controls and reimposition of import controls.

World Bank Structural Adjustment Loan

The signing of a structural adjustment loan totaling US$1 billion in September 1979 left no doubt that the political leadership publicly supported the trade and industry reforms of the 1980s. This was in marked contrast to the extended fund facility arrangement with the International Monetary Fund starting in April 1976, which included as conditions a similar set of policy reforms. In this case, however, there was much less public commitment, and very little happened in terms of implementation. What were the features of the structural adjustment loan that induced such a strong public commitment on the part of the political leadership?

The political leadership. In 1979 Roberto Ongpin became the minister of trade and industry. He came from the business ranks and was known to have access to President Ferdinand Marcos. When he supported the structural adjustment loan and its related reforms, the way was opened for the government's public endorsement. Ongpin brought with him a grand vision for industrialization. This was embodied in his so-called eleven major industrial projects—a petrochemical complex, an integrated steel mill, a copper smelter, an aluminum smelter, a phosphate fertilizer project, a diesel engine project, a cement rationalization project, an integrated pulp and paper mill, heavy engineering industries, alcogas and coconut industry rationalization—all items that the economy could ill-afford in 1979. While his ambitious programs coincided with those of the political leadership, the big problem was financing.

By 1979 the real interest rate had become positive, 1.53 percent, and it continued to rise to 2.83 percent in 1980. Prior to this, the real rate had been negative since 1975. The loan market had started to tighten and with net international reserves negative for the first time since 1973, the economy was giving clear signals of distress. A structural adjustment loan package became attractive not only for the direct loan, but because it could be construed as a vote of confidence in the future of the economy, crucial for foreign investment and private lending decisions.

Ongpin and the political leaders thought the World Bank loan could be used for their eleven major import-substituting industrial projects. The World Bank was blind to the conflict between the adjustment reforms and the eleven major industrial projects. It called a meeting for "clarification" in 1979, but was anxious to go on with the structural adjustment loan. The Philippines was among the first countries to agree to such a loan. The World Bank saw that dissent, if any, would be muted in the Philippines. The reforms in the early 1960s and 1970s were accompanied by acrimonious debates. Another reason for agreement to the structural adjustment loan was pragmatic: the economy was in deep recession.

The business sector. The business sector would be expected to oppose the structural adjustment arrangement, though not the flow of funds it engendered. This did not matter: by this time Marcos had succeeded in putting his cronies into strategic positions. He had the support of large agri-businesses. Cojuangco, Jr., the "coconut king," was riding roughshod over other businesses from his coconut-based United Cocobank. The sugar industry was ruled by "sugar king" Roberto Benedicto. "Banana king" Floreindo, dominated the banana business. The main player in the construction industry was the Construction Development Corporation of the Philippines under Rodolfo Cuenca. The Romualdezes had moved in on the Lopez group of companies. Jose Y. Campos was head of the drug companies. Fonacier presided over hotels. Lucio Tan held sway in the tremendously lucrative cigarette industry. Marcos was indeed in a position to define the industry agenda and control the economy accordingly. Those who opposed Marcos were effectively run out of the country: the Jacintos of Jacinto Steel, the Lopezes of sugar, and Meralco are examples.

The academic technocrats. Among the technocrats whom Marcos appointed, Gerardo Sicat was the one with the most well developed economic philosophy. His ideas on trade and industrial policy were presented in *New Economic Directions in the Philippines* (1974) and *The Philippines: Industrialization and Trade Policies* (1971). These volumes reflected views that resurfaced in Finance Secretary Cesar Virata's letter to the World Bank in August 1980 outlining new initiatives toward industrial restructuring. Sicat was the leader of those who felt that the Philippine economy was being left behind by its East Asian neighbors because of its inward orientation.

Marcos wrested the presidency from Macapagal who was responsible for economic decontrol (1960–1964), which in turn was publicly blamed for slowing down the investment rate in the mid-1960s and inflating the price of rice. The first Marcos era gave little room to Sicat's basic philosophy. Sicat and like-minded technocrats introduced a series of initiatives to promote exports (such as the export Incentives Act of 1968). But these did not reflect the central thrust of the economy. They were concessions to the undeniable fact of East Asian growth. The bulk of incentives continued to be for import substitution. There is a view that Marcos hired academics because the multilateral institutions were more comfortable with these technocrats and this helped facilitate loans. Political leaders then allowed the introduction of exceptions, which made a complete mockery of the spirit and letter of the plans. Sicat (1986) was only too painfully aware of this: "The development program which emanated from the planning sectors of the government had been generally of sound direction. Because the competing programs of wasteful sectors of government had edged out some funding for other more productive investment, the average productivity of government resources fell."

Academic technocrats saw a great opportunity for their ideas in the structural adjustment loan arrangements. They saw the strength of multinationals as an effective support for their views.

A happy compromise. Many groups would thus benefit from the structural adjustment loan arrangements. The International Monetary Fund could say that the extended funded facility laid the ground work for the loan; the World Bank obtained support at the cost of its muted criticism of the major projects; the academic technocrats received unprecedented financial support for their promarket ideas (Sicat faction). The business technocrats (Ongpin faction) obtained the possibility of financing for their ambitious projects. The political leadership saw its fortunes buoyed by the Ongpin projects and labeled structural adjustment the "strategy for national survival." Both the business technocrats and the political leadership saw the political cost of market reforms as skin deep if properly managed and subverted.

Implementation. In contrast to a relative buoyancy of the economy at the time of the International Monetary Fund's proposals, by 1979 the poor state of the Philippine economy transferred the focus of the structural adjustment loan arrangements away from the eleven major industrial projects component of the deal toward the reforms. (Macroeconomic statistics for the period 1976 through 1985 are presented with a commentary in the Appendix.)

Decision Making under the Aquino Government

The public agenda: University of the Philippines School of Economics. In 1984, after months of painstaking debate, a group of faculty members issued a monograph entitled *An Analysis of the Philippine Economic Crisis* (de Dios, Canlas, et al 1986). Looking at the record once more, the work conceded the adverse effects of the petroleum price increases and the barter terms-of-trade deterioration, but it also pointed out that other countries facing the same difficulties did not collapse. Domestic economic policies were basically responsible for the chronic weakness in

Philippine economic performance. The analysis carefully described the causes of Philippine difficulties. A great deal of attention was focused on rent seeking that led to collapse.

The White Paper, as the monograph was popularly known, attracted wide attention for several reasons. It was written by a group of professors who could not be associated with a single vested interest. It was not written stridently. It painstakingly argued the case without being contemptuous of alternative or opposite views. It supported its conclusions with statistics. It cited historical experiences of successful development and of failures that were all closed economies. Without being overextended, it was comprehensive. It even had a discussion of the state of data collection and processing in the Philippines. No conspiracies were revealed though rent seeking was demonstrated. The monograph expressed concern at the use of political power to reallocate economic resources. Finally, it left no doubt as to the culpability of the Marcos regime for the economic crisis.

After the June 1984 parliamentary election, central bank governor Jose B. Fernandez tried to mop up the excess liquidity that normally follows elections in the Philippines. The new measure was the sale of central bank Certificate of Indebtedness bearing record interest rates. The result was a massive squeeze on domestic production already affected by the scarcity of foreign exchange.

Another group of faculty members produced a more forward looking monograph, *Towards Recovery and Sustainable Growth* (Alburo, Canlas, et al 1985). It outlined ways to return the economy to the market: a realistic exchange rate; push for a lower average, and perhaps uniform, tariff; the lifting of nontariff barriers; and the overhaul of the investment code by abolishing such things as measured capacity, project based incentives, capital biased tax and tariff exemptions, and restrictions to entry. It also advocated measures that make the market work better, like income and asset redistribution, land reform, progressive taxes, democratization of the budget process, dismantling of monopolies, privatization, and smaller government.

This second monograph was enthusiastically promoted by the planning minister in the Aquino administration. She argued that the policies had to be implemented as a package and not in a piecemeal fashion. Monsod requested that the faculty of the School of Economics formulate a comprehensive recovery plan. The result was *Economic Recovery and Long-Run Growth: Agenda for Reforms* (Alburo, Bautista, et al 1986), composed by academics from the University of the Philippines School of Economics, University of the Philippines Los Baños and the University of the Philippines College of Public Administration and economists from the National Economic Development Authority and the Philippine Institute of Development Studies. The agenda was a reaffirmation of a competitive, market-oriented strategy that relied heavily on private enterprise. This finally became the public agenda of the Aquino government.

Implementation of the economic program of the government, however, depends on interaction between the various interested parties including the executive branch and legislative branch of government.

The executive branch. Although final decisions over sensitive issues are reached in cabinet meetings, the background spadework usually has already been done on the cabinet assistance committee level. Cabinet assistants are generally undersecretaries of the different ministries who are in theory chosen to provide technical expertise and assistance to the department secretary. The undersecretaries are largely responsible for the collection, sifting, and organization of data and information on an issue or for commissioning studies on it. They may head a technical staff who do much of this work or may be in constant contact with outside consultants hired to tackle specific issues. Many times, when more complex technical matters are involved, cabinet assistants themselves make the cabinet presentations. If an issue is not resolved at the cabinet level, it may be returned to the cabinet assistants committee for their research deliberation and negotiation. This committee is where the National Economic Development Authority exercises its oversight mandate.

Since an undersecretary usually reflects the world view of the secretary, his search for and processing of information, as well as the experts he consults, would more often than not reveal this bias. Thus the renewed focus on the car manufacturing program, which remains a hot issue, sent the participants to the Center for Research and Communication, a business-client financed research institution, which promptly called for reduced indirect taxes on cars and reduced tariffs on imported inputs as revitalization measures. This was strongly criticized in the press. Commissioned study on issues affecting business—foreign investment and comparative, Association of Southeast Asian Nations (ASEAN) incentives for example—is also done by the accounting and consulting firm, Sycip, Gorres and Velayo. Another business-oriented firm that does commissioned work is the Economic Development Foundation.

On the other hand, the agriculture secretary or undersecretaries may consult with University of the Philippines Los Baños economists on tariff reduction on fertilizer, since they have long been advocates of fertilizer market liberalization. The planning undersecretary for policy is likely to turn to the Philippine Institute of Development Studies for supporting figures on fiscal incentives to industries. In all these, if original research is nonexistent, importance is given to the record of Taiwan and Korea, and now also of Thailand. For example, there is much disagreement about the overvaluation of the currency: estimation of real effective exchange rates is difficult and can be manipulated by interested parties, namely, the National Economic Development Authority and the central bank, but reference to Thailand's exchange rate and Thailand's apparent economic health can be a convincing argument.

The problem with this is that the antagonists over an issue tend to discredit the other's figures and sources as biased. Perhaps this is why reference to other countries' experience, which is relatively unbiased, is quite effective. Even here, interpretations can vary drastically. For example, while there is broad agreement on the importance of export performance for Taiwan and Korea, how this was achieved is a subject of debate. The Philippine Chamber of Commerce and Industry and the Department of Trade and Industry argue that export performance could be improved by better government-business cooperation (say, subsidies), the elimination of bureaucratic red tape, the reduction of tax on fuel, better services and transportation, and fewer strikes. The National Economic Development Authority, on the other hand, argues that a protective regime penalizes exports and must be reformed.

When the views are irreconcilable, the debate moves into the public arena. The central bank encourages contact with columnists and other press people, and a Daily Bulletin columnist is an admitted consultant to the central bank governor. The Department of Trade and Industry arranges intensive media coverage through the Philippine Chamber of Commerce and Industries. Unionized labor was mobilized to mount mass rallies against import liberalization. A number of university academics now write for Manila dailies as either columnists or feature writers, usually in support of market forces.

An interesting case was the appearance of large amounts of imported apples on store shelves in early 1988. The opponents of import liberalization mounted a campaign of nationalism, while the academic columnists and others noted that protection of the exchange rate ought to disappear with trade reforms. In the end, the agriculture department was obliged to slow down the imports of apples.

Congress. In 1988 congress obviously attempted to define and guard, if not expand, its sphere of influence. While these powers are governed by the constitution, many details are not clear. Congress is now moving toward a re-examination of current programs, including the 1987 Omnibus Investment Code, the car program and car imports, and the debt issue. The bulk of legislative work involves committee hearings, where information is gathered, experts asked to testify, and conflicting views heard. These are open to the press and receive wide coverage. The lower house has a Congressional Economic Planning Service, which assists the congressional leadership on economic issues by gathering information, evaluating research, and consulting experts. The upper house (senate) has a budget research arm that does the same for the senate leadership. Thus the committee hearings, the Congressional Economic Planning Service, and the Budget Research Office are entry points into the congressional policy-making process. In addition, senators and congressmen work directly with academic institutions. Policy involvement is very demanding, however, and academics can quickly move out of actual research work.

Congress's record on reforms is mixed thus far, and not only are further reforms harder to push, but reforms already in place may be endangered. Congressmen, citing the interests of their constituencies, fought the attempt to raise tariffs on rubber tires. Because of complaints from bakers, the senate is investigating the cartel that virtually monopolizes flour imports. The flour import monopoly given up by a government agency, the National Food Authority, has effectively fallen into the hands of a private cartel, which means the benefit of liberalization may not filter down. This situation exists for the cement industry also. Cement importation fell into the hands of the cement manufacturers themselves. Congress is sensitive to issues of profiteering, but may not relate it in any significant way to the trade regime structure. In this regard, there is a need to monitor domestic and world prices.

One block, the "cause-oriented groups," has remained largely critical of trade reforms led by their principal research body, IBON. One area where they may have had an influence is on foreign investment policy where the 60–80 equity ownership rule holds. Another is in the price of fuel products. Consumer groups have not had an impact on tariff-related debates, but some user groups are starting to voice their concerns, the automotive parts importers for example. In the end, it is the vigor of the benefiting user group lobbies that ensures the maintenance of reforms already in place.

If it is true that liberal democratic systems with separation of powers lead to slow and protracted decision making and thus tend to favor the status quo, then the trade reforms of the 1980s stand a chance of surviving. Pushing for further reforms may, for the same reason, be more difficult. Also, if the economy avoids another balance-of-payments crisis and maintains growth, new reforms will be even less likely, although reforms in place may be harder to dislodge. If there is another balance-of-payments crisis, however, the trade reforms already in place may become scapegoats.

The Role of a Policy Research Institute

In an open society, which the Philippines aspires to be, the roles of information on the one hand and lobbying by vested interests on the other are very pronounced and often run at cross purposes. In contrast to the narrow and immediate concerns of vested interests, the role of policy research is to put issues on a global and longer term perspective. While policy research organizations need adequate financing, they must maintain a degree of independence and nonpartisanship to be effective and credible. This of course poses a dilemma. Financing usually comes from groups with a vested interest that hope to receive some return. If they are shunned, who will provide the financing? Currently, the two countries whose research is considered largely neutral are Canada and Australia. U.S. agencies are viewed with more suspicion than Japanese agencies.

The idea of a private research institute, with adequate financing (perhaps an endowment) from neutral sources, doing continuous economic policy research and monitoring was broached and is being seriously considered in the University of the Philippines School of Economics. The data bank of this institute should contain detailed information not only about the Philippines but about Korea, Taiwan, and the ASEAN economies, since reference to neighbors' experiences tends to carry strong weight with decision makers in the Philippines. Through visiting researchers, the institute could develop a comparative advantage in understanding and interpreting other countries' experiences.

Appendix

The Macroeconomic Situation, 1976–1985

Table A6.1 gives some relevant macroeconomic statistics for the extended fund facility (EFF) years (1976–1979) and the structural adjustment loan (SAL) years (1980–1985). The year 1975 is included for trend. The last two columns give the average for the four EFF years and the six SAL years where useful. During the EFF years there was an average real GNP growth rate of 6.55 percent, led by construction with 15 percent growth. Manufacturing grew by 6.45 percent. In contrast, during the SAL years the average GNP growth rate was 0.4 percent, with construction's average being –5.8 percent, and manufacturing –0.4 percent. The current-account deficit was almost US$1 billion in 1979 and was close to US$25 billion in 1982. Net international reserves became negative (–US$439 million) for the first time in 1979 and reached –$4,696 million in 1983. On average, the SAL years had a net international reserves position of –US$135 million. The net terms of trade improved

TABLE A6.1   Macroeconomic Statistics 1975–1985

	1975	1976	1977	1978	1979	1980	1981	1982	1983	1984	1985
Real GNP growth rate (%)	6.0	7.2	6.3	5.8	6.9	5.0	3.4	1.9	1.3	-5.4	-4.0
Real construction growth rate (%)	5.5	40.3	5.7	2.2	11.7	5.7	8.1	4.2	-4.8	-20.2	-28.0
Real manufacturing growth rate (%)	3.6	5.8	7.7	7.1	5.2	4.5	3.4	2.1	2.4	-7.2	-7.7
Current account deficit (Pm)	-6,071	-7,920	-4,872	-8,385	-9,763	-13,536	-15,338	-25,339	-26,394	-14,756	—
Net international reserves ($m)	324	108	249	164	-439	-811	-2,062	-3,733	-4,696	-4,251	-3,259
Net terms of trade (1972 = 100)	87.8	77.7	71.0	78.2	81.6	68.6	60.4	58.7	61.3	59.8	55.9
Crude petrol imports ($m)	712	800	861	910	1,112	1,859	2,081	1,784	1,752	1,473	1,277
Price of petroleum ($/barrel)	10.7	11.5	12.4	12.6	16.9	29.1	33.9	32.8	29.2	28.0	26.9
Consumer price index (1978 = 100)	7.0	9.6	9.9	7.1	17.6	18.2	13.0	10.3	10.0	50.3	23.1
Official exchange rate (P/US$)	7.50	7.43	7.37	7.38	7.42	7.60	8.20	9.17	14.00	19.76	19.03
Government deficit (Pm)	1,403	2,349	2,852	2,167	342	3,387	12,146	14,415	6,422	8,714	—
Incremental capital output ratio	3.60	3.34	4.65	4.89	4.43	5.54	7.31	9.75	28.49	-3.32	-8.04
Merchandise exports growth rate (%)	-15.8	12.2	22.4	8.7	34.3	25.8	-1.1	-12.3	-0.3	7.7	-14.2

SOURCE: IBRD 1987; Montes 1985.

TABLE A6.2	Debt Statistics, 1975–1985										
	1975	1976	1977	1978	1979	1980	1981	1982	1983	1984	1985
External debt rate of growth (%)	23.5	36.9	16.2	6.9	−1.8	8.3	9.9	21.9	−2.0	−2.6	5.8
Share of short-term debt to total (%)	12.8	14.0	15.3	16.4	18.5	20.8	24.6	23.5	21.0	21.0	15.5
Share of public debt to total (%)	46.5	44.6	46.1	62.2	66.1	66.8	68.7	69.8	72.9	66.5	61.2
Total debt service payment ($m)	498	858	727	1006	1253	1472	1758	2249	1896	1915	1714
International real interest rate	−2.4	−4.2	−2.7	−2.4	1.5	2.8	2.2	6.9	5.9	4.7	6.1
Critical interest rate	11.5	12.4	10.8	9.6	8.3	6.8	3.6	1.0	−12.5	−16.6	−25.0

SOURCE: Dingcong 1987.

slightly in 1979 but declined thereafter. The price of crude petroleum doubled in the SAL years, and the consumer price index also increased markedly. The official exchange rate was low until 1981, when it began to rise. The government deficit rose almost fourfold in 1981 and remained high in 1982, when the government tried to counter the recessionary effect of the second oil price rise. The incremental capital output ratio rose markedly in 1981 and continued to rise to 28 in 1983. Merchandise exports were growing well until 1981, when they began to decline.

Table A6.2 gives relevant debt statistics. Debt grew very rapidly from 1975 to 1977, decreased in 1979 and rose again until 1983. Short-term debt rose from 14 percent in 1976 to 25 percent in 1981. There was also a continuous rise in the share of public debt from 45 percent in 1976 to 73 percent in 1983, with the additional problem that many private debts had government guarantees. On average, the public share of total debt was 55 percent in the EFF years and 68 percent in the SAL years. Total debt-service payments first exceeded US$1 billion in 1978 and reached more than US$2 billion in 1982. The real international interest rate was negative from 1975 to 1978, but beginning in 1979, it was positive and rose to a high of 6.9 percent in 1982.

MANAGING ECONOMIC POLICY REFORMS IN INDONESIA

Following the chaos left by the heavily interventionist government of President Sukarno (1945–1967), the new order government of President Suharto moved to stabilize the economy and shift economic policy away from direct controls. Investment incentives for both foreign and domestic investors were introduced. After the petroleum boom of 1973 to 1982 and an increase in nationalist sentiment, foreign investment was restricted to joint ventures with specified levels of Indonesian equity. Trade and industry policies promoted import-substituting industries especially through high levels of protection, while macroeconomic policy was directed to controlling inflation.

In 1982, when petroleum prices began to fall, balance-of-payments problems emerged and there was a reduction in government revenue for development expenditure. Austerity measures, tax reforms, and banking deregulation were introduced, but at the same time, there was an increase in trade protection, which had the aim of stimulating domestic industry and saving foreign exchange. It was not until 1985–1986 that the deteriorating economic situation made it politically feasible to introduce major reforms. Current deregulation includes reforms to remove the bias against exports and to encourage foreign investment. Liberalization of capital markets and the financial sector is also proceeding.

Policies are coordinated by the Ministry of Economic Coordination. All cabinet-level departments have a research organization, but there is often a lack of researchers and poor coordination of research activities. Although reform proposals are usually initiated by a core group of economic ministers, the National Planning Agency and outside consultants also have important input to policy research and development. Under the new order government, crises were met with the following policy sequence: macroeconomic stabilization, then resource mobilization, and then measures to reduce costs or increase efficiency. The consistency of economic management is attributable to a stable core of economic ministers working closely together. Most policy input is transmitted through internal government channels, and public debate is limited, although recently there has been a recognition of the role of the press and business associations in economic policy debate.

Indonesian experience suggests that major changes in the direction of trade and industrial policy are linked to major political and economic crises. Although the need for reforms may be recognized among groups both within and outside the government for some time, the political will necessary to undertake reforms usually comes from major political and economic crises. In the early period of 1967–1972, the impetus for reforms was a change in government. In the recent period, 1982–1989, reform was motivated by the rapid decline in the price of petroleum, which resulted in a need to increase the role of private sector investment and to expand nonpetroleum exports.

The aim of this chapter is to analyze episodes of economic policy reform in Indonesia, especially from 1982 to 1989, and evaluate the factors, especially the role of policy research, that led to the reforms. In this context trade reforms are interpreted as policies that affect exports and imports directly, while industrial reforms affect the industrial structure of the economy through investment decisions or direction of market orientation, that is, import substitution or export promotion. Changes in macroeconomic policy, especially exchange-rate management, are also included because they are part of the general restructuring strategy. Even though substantive trade and industry reforms were undertaken in the early years of the new order government, the focus in this chapter will be on the more recent period of reforms.

The chapter begins with a brief look at policy in the new order period, 1967–1981, and moves on to a brief overview of policy making in Indonesia. Following this is an analysis of the process of policy reform during the period of petroleum price declines, 1982–1989. The components of the analysis are identification of the need for reform, recommended solutions and alternatives, expected costs and benefits, arrangements for implementation and enforcement, transition problems, and the impact of reforms to date. The analysis does not pretend to be comprehensive since the decision-making process is complex. Unfortunately many questions remain unanswered at this stage because it is difficult to confirm how the process works in practice and implementation is often at variance with the formal process. The chapter concludes by making recommendations on improving the process of policy making, and discussing the role of policy research as an input into the process.

Policy Direction in the New Order Period, 1967–1981

Identifiable periods of protectionism and liberalization are closely linked to major economic and political changes. Liberalization, at least until recently, often appeared to be ad hoc rather than part of a systematic plan. A summary of these changes in policy direction and economic conditions is given in Table 7.1.

Stabilization, 1967–1972. The new order government carried out a substantial economic liberalization program, which included trade and industrial reforms. This policy approach contrasted sharply with the heavily interventionist policies of the Sukarno government. The influence of western-trained economists, together with reactions to both the economic chaos left by the old government and the corruption that accompanied public intervention in the economy, pushed the new order government away from direct controls and toward economic policy. An open capital account with no foreign-exchange controls was introduced. The multiple exchange-rate system was unified in 1970, and the rupiah was devalued in 1971. As the focus shifted toward increasing domestic production, tariffs on some products were increased in 1968. Production increased, notably in the textile industry, not only due to protection but also as a result of an open-door investment policy.

The 1967 Foreign Investment Law aimed to restore investor confidence and encourage private investment in priority sectors. It included a package of incentives: tax holidays, import duty and sales tax exemption on imports of machinery and equipment, accelerated depreciation, guaranteed repatriation of capital and profits, and provisions to carry losses forward. After a lot of persuasion the same benefits were extended to domestic investors under the 1968 Domestic Investment Law. Initially there were no restrictions on foreign equity and employment of expatriates, and 100 percent foreign ownership was allowed. The only restriction on foreign investors was that they were not allowed to distribute their own products in the domestic market.

The process of change was smooth and relatively swift since the new order government was concerned with restoring and rehabilitating an economy that had been producing at 20 to 30 percent of capacity, had a badly damaged economic and physical infrastructure, very low levels of trade, negligible foreign-exchange reserves, and hyperinflation. The

TABLE 7.1   **Economic Reforms**

Reform	1967–1972 Stabilization period	1973–1981 Petroleum boom years	1982–1985 Ambivalent period	1986–1989 Deregulation phase
Macro				
Fiscal			Tax reform, 1984	Continued tax reform
Monetary		Use of credit ceilings and credit allocation Limited monetary control	Introduction of new monetary instruments	Improved monetary instruments
Foreign exchange	Unified exchange rate, 1970 Devaluation, 1971	Devaluation, 1978 Central bank swap, 1979	Devaluation, 1983	Devaluation, 1985 Removal of swap ceiling, 1986 Swap premium flex., 1988
Investment	Open door policy—liberal except for domestic distribution	Increased restrictions on ownership and priority list Capital limits Administrative reform		Increased foreign ownership permitted (95%) Access to export credit for export-oriented firms Liberalized domestic distribution Deregulation of investment licensing and renewal

Trade

Protection	Tariff main instrument	Increased nontariff barriers	From nontariff barriers to tariff
Neutralize	Tariff reduction, 1979 Duty drawback, 1978	Tariff reform, 1985 Customs reform, 1985 Shipping deregulation, 1985	Improved duty drawback, 1986 Improved textile quota allocation, 1987
Promotion		Export credit, 1982	
Financial	Open entry	Closed Deregulation of interest rates, 1983 Removal of credit ceilings	Open to new entry Deregulation of insurance and capital markets

change in political power removed entrenched interests, which are all too often an obstacle to reform.

Petroleum boom years, 1973–1982. The petroleum boom that began with the quadrupling of petroleum prices in 1973 and continued until 1982, dulled much of the government's resolve to institute reforms that would provide a greater role for the private sector. Instead there were more protectionist and interventionist policies.

Regulations regarding foreign investment became more restrictive. The open-door policy for foreign investment and the first phase of import substitution in final goods had led to a surge of foreign investment responding to the incentives. The concentration of Japanese investment in the highly visible consumer products sector led to strong anti-Japanese riots during the visit of Prime Minister Kakuei Tanaka in 1974. (In fact, the value of U.S. investment was much higher, but it was concentrated in the less visible, capital-intensive petroleum sector.)

In the aftermath, restrictions that reflected increased nationalist sentiments were placed on foreign investment. All new foreign investments were to be in the form of joint ventures, Indonesian equity was to be increased within a specified period, the list of closed sectors was extended, tax incentives were reduced, and the number of expatriate employees restricted. After much complaint from investors, however, the administrative procedures for investment applications were simplified in 1977, and the Board of Investment was made a "one stop service" so that an investor did not have to obtain approvals from other government departments. But during the second petroleum boom in 1979, foreign- investment requirements were tightened once more by making the priority list more restrictive.

Trade and industrial policies during this period were directed at influencing the pattern of industrialization by protecting domestic industries. As other developing countries have done, Indonesia adopted an import-substitution strategy beginning with final consumer goods and then moving to intermediate and capital goods. The regime that developed was characterized by escalating protection through tariff and nontariff barriers, high and variable effective rates of protection biased against export production, proliferation of administrative procedures, and excessive government intervention.

Macroeconomic policy, however, was fairly sound during the new order period. It was characterized by prudent fiscal policy and a concern for controlling inflation. Prudent fiscal policy is reflected in the balanced budget rule and in the fact that Indonesia did not borrow as heavily as other oil-producing countries. The conservative foreign borrowing policy was related to both a rule of thumb that the debt-service ratio should not be above 22 percent and caution resulting from the

Pertamina crisis, in which Pertamina, the state oil company, incurred debts on the order of US$10 billion.

The government was less successful in controlling inflation. The substantial increase in money supply due to the spending of oil revenues could not be sterilized with the limited monetary instruments available. High inflation, around 20 percent per year, resulted. This increase contributed to a reversal of the terms of trade for non-oil goods, in response to which the rupiah was devalued. The 50 percent devaluation of the rupiah in 1978 showed the government's willingness to react quickly to a change in economic conditions with appropriate real exchange-rate management.

Overview of Policy Making

The process of making policy decisions has three aspects: the formal decision-making process; the sources of policy input both within the government and outside; and the process of transmission, from policy input to policy makers.

The decision-making process. The formal decision-making process involves the relevant ministries at various levels and coordination between ministries. Technically, the process is supposed to be from the bottom up—that is, the idea for changes should be developed at either the directorate or bureau level. The idea for change itself could come from the directorate in question. It would be formulated and discussed in an interdepartmental forum at a lower level before going to higher levels. The idea could also come from the top and be delegated to the lower levels for formulation and packaging.

The main government ministries involved in economic policy reforms can be divided into those with and those without a technical department. Those without technical departments (state ministries) concentrate on planning and policy formulation and do not implement policies, whereas ministries with a technical department (line ministries) implement policies at various levels of government. There are also such nonministerial agencies as the central bank. Three major areas of policy—economics, people's welfare, and politics and security—are coordinated by coordinating ministries. In Figure 7.1, it can be seen that the line of authority goes from the various government ministries directly to the president.

The state ministries involved in economic policy making include the Cabinet Ministry for Promotion of the Use of Domestic Products (1983–1988), the Ministry of Research and Technology, and the Ministry of Environment and Population. There are nine industries, mainly high-tech

FIGURE 7.1   Policy-Making Organization and Inputs

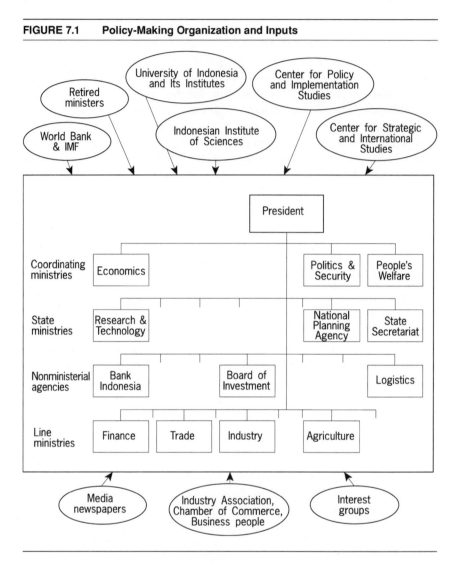

industries such as aircraft, that are under the Ministry of Research and Technology. Line ministries involved in economic policy include the Ministry of Finance, Ministry of Trade, Ministry of Industry, and Ministry of Agriculture. Other government agencies involved in economic policy are the National Planning Agency (BAPPENAS), the Logistics Agency, and the central bank (Bank Indonesia).

All economic policy is coordinated by the Ministry of Economic Coordination. Technically there are eighteen government departments and four government agencies under this ministry. Although the actual involvement of government ministries depends on the policy in question, the main ministries and government agencies involved in economic policy are the Ministry of Finance, the Ministry of Trade, the Ministry of Industry, Bank Indonesia, and the National Planning Agency.

Technically, ministers can issue ministerial decrees, but policies are usually discussed and approved at economic coordination meetings, which are held on a regular basis. Typically, the minister of economic coordination will also seek a presidential recommendation before the actual implementation of the ministerial decree. If the decree is a joint ministerial decree, then all relevant ministries must approve it. Agreement is reached through interdepartmental meetings as well as economic coordination meetings. The minister of economic coordination is clearly a key player in the process.

Technically, the relevant ministries must obtain presidential approval for a presidential decree or instruction. Ministries will often use the forum of economic coordination meetings and seek the support of the minister of economic coordination before initiating this process. Policy recommendations must be channeled through the cabinet secretary at the State Secretariat.

Sources of policy input. For an outsider who has not been involved in the policy-making process it is difficult to describe the process and draw conclusions about the relative strengths of different contributors. Hence, the following attempts to describe the main sources of inputs to policy making without evaluating their relative importance.

Every department has a research body within its own ministry to provide inputs to the other directorates. Thus when a reform is being considered the departmental research body would formulate the policy in consultation with relevant technical directorates in its own and other ministries. The Appendix gives a detailed description of the structure of the main economic ministries.

The policy-making input of research institutions within ministries varies among ministries and between reforms. The crucial obstacles to this input are lack of researchers and lack of coordination within and among ministries. It is probably fair to generalize that in most cases research bodies in ministries have had some input, and outside consultants have had an important role only in packaging reforms, not in suggesting the need for reforms. Furthermore, credit for the origin of the idea and the need for reform should be given to technocrat economic ministers. The core group of economic ministers has worked closely together for most of the new order period. New ministers often have experience with the group. Their common links are postgraduate training in economics in the west and affiliation with the Faculty of Economics at the University of Indonesia.

In addition to the research departments of the various ministries, the National Planning Agency is expected to act as a think tank on economic issues and planning with a concomitant responsibility for initiating change.

Input into policy making also comes from outside the government, from multilateral agencies, domestic and foreign consultants, independent research agencies, and academics. Nongovernment think tanks have not had a major influence in economic policy reform, although they have provided background research and general policy input. There are several research institutions with some policy input:

- The Social and Economic Research Institute (LPEM, Lembaga Penelitian Ekonomi Masyarakat), The Management Institute (LM, Lembaga Manajemen), and The Institute of Demography (LD, Lembaga Demografi) are government institutions operated by the Faculty of Economics of the University of Indonesia. These organizations often do consulting for the government on a contract basis, but not specifically for policy reform.

- The Center for Policy and Implementation Studies (CPIS) is a semigovernmental research institution under the Ministry of Finance that focuses on rural finance, the informal sector, education, and agriculture.

- The Indonesian Institute of Sciences (LIPI, Lembaga Ilmu Pengetahuan Indonesia) is the government research agency in various sciences, including economics. It does contract as well as other policy research.

- The Center for Strategic and International Studies (CSIS) is a private research institution that works on economics, politics, and sociocultural issues. CSIS conducts policy-related research in a number of areas—among them are industrialization, energy, and trade.

The rigorous quantification of costs and benefits, conceptualization of alternatives, packaging of reforms, and measurement of their impact have been undertaken by various groups of foreign consultants as well as by such multilateral agencies as the World Bank and the International Monetary Fund. This preference for foreign consultants can be explained by a desire for confidentiality as well as by the shortage of qualified domestic consultants.

Multilateral institutions, mainly the World Bank, have made significant policy inputs. The World Bank mission in Indonesia has the largest nonlocal staff of any World Bank country mission. Every year the World Bank produces a special thematic study and a country report containing recommendations for structural change. The country report is used as a basis for discussions by Indonesia's donor countries at the Inter-Governmental Group on Indonesia (IGGI) meetings every year. This report is submitted after discussions with various economic and related ministries. The International Monetary Fund also has some input, especially in the area of macroeconomic stabilization policy.

The longest standing group of foreign consultants is from the Harvard Institute for International Development (HIID), which has been under contract to the government since 1969. Other consulting agencies composed of foreign academics as well as the larger international consulting companies have also been retained.

Although there are quite a number of private domestic consulting firms, there are no substantive groups that make significant policy inputs. Because the ministers and many of the senior officials come from the universities, it is also quite common that other university professors, either informally or formally, provide inputs. This process, however, is not regular or continuous and is very much personality driven.

Finally, an important policy input of a noninstitutional nature is the role of former government officials, sometimes ministers, who are retained in an advisory capacity.

The transmission process. Most of the policy input provided by the above sources is confidentially transmitted from the source to the user through commissioned reports and memoranda. The role of public debate is limited; the main institutional channels are the House of Representatives and the press. Business interests use business or industry associations, particularly the Chamber of Commerce and Industry. Various ministries seek informal input from the business sector. MacIntyre (1988) points out that the role of the House of Representatives is often underestimated. Although the Indonesian Parliament cannot be considered a strong voice in the policy-making process and has not yet exercised its constitutional power to initiate legislation, it has had some influence through the various committees within the House of Representatives by delaying or forcing changes in government legislation. Policy debates in committee hearings on particular issues are also important. Committees cannot force officials to provide information or cooperate, but since there is wide press coverage of these hearings, government officials take them seriously.

The press operates under formal and informal censorship. There is also self-censorship and an understanding that certain sensitive issues are not to be reported. Nevertheless, press commentary and letters to the editor play an important role in public debate, and government officials are sensitive to press coverage.

A case in point was the closure of Sinar Harapan not long after the September 1986 devaluation. The reason for closure was a perception that the newspaper exercised a lack of self-censorship regarding economic issues that could have worsened the crisis of confidence in government economic management caused by the devaluation. There were two main reports that caused problems. First, an economist recommended that privately owned deposits be converted to government bonds, which, instead of foreign loans, would be used to finance the government deficit; this caused a light run on deposits and was perceived to add to the crisis in confidence. Second, a draft proposal for substantive trade reforms, including removal of the controversial import monopolies, was leaked. The two explanations that emerged for this leak indicate the potential role of press coverage as a forum for influencing policy changes: one explanation was that the proposal was leaked by those in the government wishing to push the reforms, and the other was that it was leaked by those who wanted to kill the reforms.

The role of business associations as a means of communication is also important. There are hundreds of government-approved business associations, and the umbrella organization for about two-thirds of these is the Chamber of Commerce and Industry. Because of its close ties to the government, the common perception is that the chamber has not been influential in promoting business interests. Nevertheless, some private sector business associations do promote the interests of their members. An example is the Spinning Industry Joint Secretariat, which successfully mounted a campaign between 1986 and 1988 to have the import monopoly removed. Apart from direct lobbying, the industry association also used press coverage to achieve its aims (MacIntyre 1988, ch. 4).

Policy Making and Deregulation, 1982–1989

Reforms must be seen as part of the restructuring strategy carried out in response to falling petroleum prices. In this section the content and sequencing of policy reforms will be analyzed, as will the importance of macroeconomic stability in facilitating successful reforms. A summary of the reform measures and effects are given in Table 7.2.

Falling petroleum prices had important implications for Indonesia. There was a fall in foreign-exchange earnings. Appreciation of the yen, especially after 1985, worsened the balance-of-payments situation since

TABLE 7.2   Reforms and Effects, 1983–1988

Date and reform	Contents	Effects
March 1983 Devaluation	50% devaluation	
June 1983 Banking deregulation	Deposit interest rates for state banks decontrolled	Rise in deposit interest rate
	Liquidity credits reduced	Some fall in intermediation costs
	Credit ceilings removed	
April 1984 Tax reform	VAT introduced	Some increase in government revenues
	Income and sales tax rationalized	
March 1985 Tariff reform	Tariff range reduced from 0–225% to 0–60%	Reduced protection
	Number of tariff levels reduced from 25 to 11	Rationalization of tariff system
April 1985 Customs reform	Swiss company replaces customs officials	Time and cost of importing and exporting reduced
	Restrictions on choice of carrier for international shipment removed	Powerful signal
May 1986 Customs reform	New duty drawback and partial import monopoly bypass	Improved duty drawback process
	Arm's length transactions and computerized processing	
	Up to 95% foreign ownership of export-oriented joint ventures permitted	
	Restrictions on domestic distribution by export-oriented firms relaxed	
	Joint ventures permitted to utilize export credit	
September 1986 Devaluation	50% devaluation	Increase in non-oil exports
		Improved balance-of-payments deficit
		Small confidence crisis
October 1986 and January 1987	Number of goods subject to import licensing reduced	Improvement of investment climate
		Increase in investment, especially export-oriented

continued on next page

TABLE 7.2 continued

Date and reform	Contents	Effects
Deregulation	Decrease in tariffs for items facing nontariff barriers Tariffs on inputs reduced Ceiling on central bank swap facility removed	
June 1987 Investment	Investment and capacity licensing deregulated Closed sectors opened to export-oriented firms	Improvement of investment climate and increase in investment
July 1987 Textile quota reform	Transparency of allocation	Increase in exports of textiles and garments
December 1987 Capital market reforms	Capital markets deregulated Government role in stock exchange reduced Foreigners permitted to buy stocks Tourism and hotel sector deregulation Export-oriented firm more loosely defined	Increase in exports of textiles and garments No significant effect on capital market by early 1989
October 1988 Financial deregulation	Restrictions on entry into banking removed and foreign joint ventures permitted Lending limit regulations	3 new banking joint ventures 17 new banks Increased banking competition Rising interest rates and falling spreads
November 1988 Trade deregulation	Removal of import monopolies for plastics and steel Shipping deregulation Foreign investors allowed to distribute products domestically	Positive sign of seriousness of government apparent Some inconsistencies Improved investment climate
December 1988 Capital market deregulation	Capital markets deregulated further Insurance deregulated Financial services rationalized	Sharp increase in capital market activity but market remains small

TABLE 7.3   **Financing Sources of the Development Budget,**
1969–70 to 1987–88

	Government saving[a]		Foreign borrowing		Development budget
	Billions of Rp.	%	Billions of Rp.	%	(billions of Rp.)
First Five-Year Development Plan					
1969–70	27.2	23.0	91.0	77.0	118.2
1970–71	56.4	31.9	120.4	68.1	176.8
1971–72	78.9	36.8	135.5	63.2	214.4
1972–73	152.5	49.2	157.8	50.9	310.3
1973–74	254.4	55.5	203.9	44.5	458.3
Second Five-Year Development Plan					
1974–75	737.6	76.1	232.0	23.9	969.6
1975–76	909.3	64.9	491.6	35.1	1400.9
1976–77	1276.2	62.0	783.8	38.1	2060.0
1977–78	1386.5	64.2	773.4	35.8	2159.9
1978–79	1522.4	59.2	1035.5	40.8	2557.9
Third Five-Year Development Plan					
1979–80	2635.0	65.6	1381.1	34.4	4016.1
1980–81	4427.0	74.8	1493.8	25.2	5920.8
1981–82	5235.0	73.8	1709.0	26.6	6944.0
1982–83	5422.0	73.7	1940.0	26.4	7362.0
1983–84	6020.9	60.8	3882.4	39.2	9903.3
Fourth Five-Year Development Plan					
1984–85	6476.5	65.1	3478.0	34.9	9954.5
1985–86	7301.3	67.2	3572.6	32.9	10873.9
1986–87[b]	2581.3	31.0	5752.2	69.0	8335.5
1987–88[c]	2209.6	28.5	5547.0	71.5	7756.6

a. Includes excess budgeted balance.
b. Realized figures.
c. Budgeted figures.
SOURCE: Indonesia, *State Budget, 1987–88.*

around one-third of Indonesia's foreign debt is denominated in yen. Furthermore, around 60 percent of government revenue came from taxes on petroleum corporations, and due to this, there was a substantial fall in government revenue available for development expenditure. Table 7.3 shows that government savings increased rapidly during the petroleum boom years, but then fell substantially beginning in 1986.

In the initial period of the oil price decline, the government response was ambivalent. While the need for resource mobilization, increasing foreign-exchange reserves through promotion of non-oil exports, and increasing the role of the private sector were recognized, it took some time before political will became strong enough to push policy reforms. It was not until oil prices fell to US$10 a barrel in 1986 that it became politically feasible to implement several of the policy reforms that had been present in the political debates for some time.

The ambivalent period, 1982–1985. *Devaluation and austerity measures.* The government responded quickly in terms of exchange-rate management and austerity measures. In March 1983 the rupiah was devalued by 50 percent. The devaluation was only undertaken after a significant capital outflow due to speculation regarding the possibility of devaluation due to the oil price decline. Nevertheless, devaluation helped increase the nominal value of government revenues in rupiah terms despite the decline in oil revenues. The devaluation was also couched in terms of increasing non-oil exports, but since the devaluation was not accompanied by the much needed deregulation in the export sector and was in fact accompanied by increased protectionist policies, the effect of devaluation was soon eroded.

Austerity measures came in the form of budget cuts and increased efforts to prevent leakages. In 1983 several capital- and import-intensive projects were postponed. Subsidies on domestic fuel, agriculture, and state enterprises were reduced and eventually removed. More attention was also given to the disbursement of funds borrowed abroad, with a commission being set up to look into the issue; undisbursed funds as a budgetary item was also removed.

Resource mobilization efforts. The government also moved quickly in efforts to increase mobilization of domestic funds from the financial sector and improve collection of non-oil tax revenues. Significant financial and fiscal reforms were implemented with the 1983 banking deregulation and the tax reforms of 1984. In an effort to increase the efficiency of the banking system and mobilize funds, credit ceilings were abolished, liquidity credits were reduced, and state banks were allowed to set their own interest rates on deposits. The tax reform was aimed at improving the collection of tax revenues from non-oil sources. The reform was undertaken in stages beginning in 1984 with the abolition of the withholding tax and the introduction of the value-added tax. Subsequently income and sales taxes were rationalized.

Increased protection: nontariff barriers. In contrast to financial measures, trade and industrial policies were not liberalized but became more protectionist. Quantitative restrictions on imports were increased under the approved importers system (Tata Niaga Impor) introduced in 1982. Prior to this importers who obtained a license from the Department of Trade were either general importers who could import most goods or importer-producers who imported raw materials and intermediate goods necessary in their production. Quantitative restrictions took the form of explicit import quotas—on foreign films, powdered milk, and for some period of time, raw cotton—and bans—on Chinese printed matter, drugs, chemicals, and fully assembled motor vehicles and motorcycles. Imports of powdered milk by milk processing plants and of raw cotton by spinning factories was tied to a fixed ratio of domestic supply.

Under the approved importer system introduced in 1982, goods listed in nine categories—electrical and electronic goods, chemical products, metal industry products, machinery and spare parts, heavy equipment and spare parts, motor vehicle components, textiles, agricultural products, and food, beverages, and fresh fruits—could be imported only by approved importers. Exceptions were made for imports under the foreign and domestic investment laws, foreign aid agreements, government projects, service contracts, and production sharing contracts. Initially two types of licenses were issued. Under the first type, general licenses (*importer umum*), an importer is approved to import goods falling in certain categories; an additional, specific import license for each batch of imports is not necessary, and the amount, type, and country of origin of the goods are not specified. In spite of this, the government can limit the number of approved importers to those that satisfy certain criteria, such as past performance and the hiring of skilled labor. These criteria, however, were never made clear. At least on paper, importers are granted approval for two years, but they must report their realized imports every three to six months.

The second type of licenses were discretionary or specific, aimed at controlling the amount and type of goods entering the economy. Approved importers were eligible to apply for a license to import goods, which may or may not be automatically approved. The type or amount of goods imported was specified, which made this a de facto quota system. It was possible for the government to specify a zero amount or to disallow an import license.

Under the approved importer system more goods were delegated to state trading and producing enterprises for importation. Before this system was introduced, imports of cement, fertilizers, and some processed agricultural products such as wheat flour and cooking oil were imported by state enterprises. The main motivation had been price stabilization of strategic commodities by ensuring adequate supplies, but another reason was protection of government-owned corporations producing cement, flour, and fertilizers. The reasons goods were added to this list appear to be protection of domestic industries considered capable of satisfying demand, protection of state-owned corporations, and conservation of foreign exchange. The additions included steel, scrap metal, tires, tin plates, and plastic raw materials.

The purported objective of the approved importer system was a combination of protection and foreign-exchange saving. Press releases and interviews with officials involved in the process, however, indicated that another underlying objective was to increase the professionalism of importers. It was not the idea of the system's originators that quantitative restrictions should develop. The idea was more to streamline imports, and a bona fide importer could import all nine categories of products under the general importer category. Nevertheless, in the period 1982–1986, especially 1983–1984, many licenses of the second type were issued. In addition to direct balance-of-payments pressures, there was renewed support for import-substitution industrialization aimed at intermediate and upstream products such as iron, steel, synthetic fibers, cement, chemicals, fertilizers, and motor vehicle engines. The underlying argument was that such an industrialization strategy would relieve balance-of-payments problems. Tariff levels were already high, but did not provide the required protection. Instead of increasing tariffs, nontariff barriers were increased because they were less visible.

As a result, several types of import licenses other than the general import licenses were developed for

- importer/producers, who needed to import raw materials or intermediate goods (*importir produsen*)

- agents licensed to import a particular brand of products (*agent tunggal*)

- producer/importers or producers who were the only ones approved to import products that they were also producing (*produsen importir*), such as Giwang Selogam on behalf of Krakatau Steel, the state-owned steel mill, which imports all steel products

- the import of certain goods, for example plastic raw materials such as polyesterene and polyethylene, which was designated to one or a number of the state trading companies (*importir terbatas*)

It was estimated for 1986 that 28 percent of the total number of items imported, 26 percent of the total import value, and 31 percent of value added were restricted under the approved importer system.

An important development during this period was the 1983 creation of the Cabinet Ministry for Promotion of the Use of Domestic Products (*Promosi Pendayagunaan Produk Dalam Negeri*). This ministry was given the task of increasing the use of domestic products, notably intermediate goods, as part of the industrialization strategy, thus enhancing the protectionist trend. There was an increase in nontariff barriers and in domestic component or localization policies.

The approval process regarding the second category of import licenses provides some insight to the process of policy making. The list of goods to be imported under this system, the amount of imports allowed, and sometimes the fixed selling price of the product (such as steel products) are determined after a discussion between an interdepartmental team made up of the Ministries of Finance, Trade, Industry, and Promotion of the Use of Domestic Products (until the termination of this ministry in the new 1988 cabinet), business, and industry groups. Examples of manufactured products affected are piston rings, automotive components, milk products, steel, white cement, inner tire tubes, some dyes, heavy equipment, PVC, motor vehicle tire tubes, hand sprayers, batik, textiles, and glass sheets.

In theory a domestic industry that can show it can produce a given product in sufficient quantity and of acceptable quality at a price competitive with imports can petition for a limitation on competing imports through the interdepartmental team. The process is that the petition, which can come from an individual producer or from an industry association, will first be lodged with the relevant technical directorate in the Ministry of Industry. The officials evaluate the petition by using information from the applicant, information from the users or consumers of the product, and their own information as well as discussions with relevant officials in the other ministries. A rough rule of the thumb is that the domestic price is competitive with imports if it is less than or equal to 15 percent more than the import price. The interdepartmental team can consider import restrictions if the customs duty does not exceed 20 percent, agreement between producers and consumers is reached, and the restrictions are temporary insofar as they can be lifted any time there are supply shortages or price instability.

Despite the trend toward increased protectionism during the mid-1980s, two important and substantive reforms were undertaken with respect to tariffs and customs procedures near the end of the initial petroleum price decline period. This marked the beginning of the deregulation drive stemming from the petroleum price decline. It was directed at increasing nonpetroleum exports, increasing the efficiency of the economy, and increasing participation by the private sector.

It is important to note that the problem of the "high-cost economy"—high costs due to protection, inefficiencies in the processing of government related regulations, and the inevitable abuses inherent in a highly regulated system—was recognized long before the actual reforms were undertaken. The high-cost economy problem received wide press coverage. Studies measuring the high and variable rates and distortionary nature of protection were undertaken by the World Bank, other foreign consultants hired by the government, as well as the research institutes attached to the universities.

The 1985 tariff reforms. In 1985 the tariff system was rationalized substantially by an across-the-board reduction in the range and level of nominal tariffs. The range of tariffs was reduced from 0–225 percent to 0–60 percent, with most tariffs in the 5–35 percent range. The number of tariff levels was also reduced from twenty-five to eleven. Despite the increase in nontariff barriers during this period, the rationalization of tariffs must be viewed as a positive development.

The push toward reducing tariffs was already evident in the late 1970s and early 1980s. In fact, in April 1979, in the wake of the 1978 devaluation, the tariffs on a thousand goods were reduced by 50 percent, and the number of imports subject to a specific tariff was increased for luxury items. Nevertheless, many of the goods that had their tariffs reduced, experienced subsequent tariff increases as protectionist tendencies predominated. Preparations for an across-the-board tariff reform along the lines of the 1979 tariff reductions were undertaken in the early 1980s by the research departments in the Ministries of Industry, Trade, and Finance. Despite cabinet changes in 1983, the ministers and the coordinating minister were in agreement. The problem was timing: falling petroleum prices and weak domestic demand made the arguments for reducing protection politically unacceptable. What finally made the reforms acceptable in 1985 was linking them to the tax reforms of 1984. The argument was that a rationalization of the tariff system was needed to make it consistent with the new value-added tax.

Awareness of the problems of high and variable rates of protection, distortionary effects of protection, inefficiencies of domestic industries, and the export bias certainly existed at the time. The World Bank and the Harvard Institute of International Development undertook several detailed and comprehensive studies quantifying the effects of protection in the early 1980s. In spite of this awareness, there was a time lag of several years before substantive reforms were made.

Customs and shipping reforms. In April 1985 all operations relating to the import and export of goods by the customs department were totally disbanded in the bold sweep of Presidential Instruction No. 4. The reform was undertaken in order to reduce the discretionary powers of customs officials. This had long been recognized as a major problem and was often cited as an important element in Indonesia's high-cost economy. Customs officials were replaced by a private Swiss surveying company, Société Générale de Surveillance (SGS), who cleared goods for import at the point of importation. Estimation of the duty rate and value of imports is done at the point of origin of the goods and the importer pays the duty directly to his bank. Therefore, there was a reduction in the number of customs officials and discretion used at the point of entry. Other parts of Presidential Instruction No. 4 deregulated interisland transportation by reducing documentation, rationalizing port fees, and allowing foreign carriers to operate.

There appear to have been few transitionary problems, and in effect the change happened overnight. The customs officials whose services were not required were either shifted to other jobs or given early retirement with the normal official compensation. It is widely accepted and acclaimed that the average time spent on customs procedures has been cut by several weeks and that the cost of shipping exports and imports has fallen substantially.

It is evident once again that although problems associated with customs procedures had long been recognized, as indicated by the open debate that occurred in the media, reforms took time. In this case, it was realized that it would be difficult to correct the existing institutional arrangements and the alternative chosen was to replace it completely. The idea of using a private surveyor company is not completely new; it has been used by other countries. Given that many people were to be laid off and that it was essentially a privatization move, the fact that such a bold move was accepted indicates that the will to undertake reforms was beginning to be felt.

The deregulation phase, 1986–1989. The sharp decline in petroleum prices that occurred in 1986 marked the turning point in the present phase of deregulation. Ironically the decline in petroleum revenues and the deteriorating balance-of-payments situation provided the political will for substantive deregulation to take place. Indonesia is at the beginning of a deregulation process and an export-oriented strategy. At this stage deregulation is usually aimed at removing the bias against exports caused by the prevailing system of protection rather than removing the source of distortions.

The May 1986 package: removing export bias and encouraging foreign investment. The first step in reducing costs for exporters was the customs cleanup in 1985. Subsequent deregulations aimed at offsetting costs to exporters either by simplification of procedures or by allowing exporters special facilities and by slowly dismantling the system of protection by changing from nontariff barriers to tariffs, which are considered to cause fewer distortions.

The 1986–1987 period can be seen to be one where the resolve to deregulate was very strong. In May 1986 a new and improved duty drawback system was introduced. Exporters can obtain a refund on the duty paid on imports used to produce exports; they are also allowed to bypass the import monopolies as long as the import is used in export production. The old export certificate scheme introduced in 1978 was found to have an export subsidy component, and since Indonesia became a signatory to the General Agreement on Tariffs and Trade (GATT) Code on Subsidies and Countervailing Duties in 1985, the system had to be changed. Exporters were defined to be producers who exported 85 percent or more of their total production. The unique feature of the new system is that applicants for duty drawback are not allowed to meet the officials processing their applications. Applications must be sent by mail or courier and all enquiries are to be made by telephone. The computerized and arm's length application procedures were designed to reduce the abuses that existed in the old system.

Other important features of the new regulations were that exporting foreign investment firms could have up to 95 percent foreign ownership and could utilize low-interest export credit, and that joint ventures with 75 percent or more Indonesian equity could undertake domestic distribution.

The September 1986 devaluation. The next spate of deregulation came after the September 1986 devaluation. Unlike the other devaluations (1978 and 1983), this devaluation was considered successful in terms of increasing nonpetroleum exports, because it controlled inflation (the rate of inflation was around 9 percent during 1987) and the deregulation measures undertaken. Real effective exchange rates thus remained competitive and deregulation not only reduced costs in the economy, but also indicated that the government was serious about improving producers' regulatory environment.

The results to date are encouraging. Nonpetroleum exports have increased substantially. Manufactured products had an annual growth rate of 57 percent in 1987. The share of nonpetroleum exports has also increased from 31 percent to 50 percent between 1978 and 1987, and the share of manufactured exports in total nonpetroleum exports has increased from 6 percent to 49 percent during the same period. Future growth of nonpetroleum exports will depend on further deregulation as well as new investment and the implementation of ongoing deregulation.

Following the devaluation there were several important policy packages aimed at improving the investment climate and increasing nonpetroleum exports. In the October 1986 and January 1987 deregulation packages the number of goods imported under the approved importer system was reduced and replaced by tariffs. The ceiling on the swap facility with Bank Indonesia was also removed.

Investment deregulation. In June 1987 the investment and capacity licensing requirement for domestic firms was substantially deregulated. Prior to deregulation renewal (varying between two and five years) and expansion in capacity necessitated reapplication to the Department of Industry. Under the new regulations renewal is no longer necessary, and only expansion of capacity exceeding 30 percent needs approval. Furthermore, the categorization of licenses was considerably broadened in order to encourage diversification within the same type of product. Previously closed sectors can now be opened if an investor is export oriented, that is, exporting 85 percent or more of production.

Rationalization of textile quotas. In July 1987 the system of textile quota allocation to Indonesian exporters was also improved. The main changes aimed at reducing the discretionary powers of officials and unnecessary administrative procedures and costs. The initial allocation is still based on past performance; the main difference is that allocations are published in the media by company and allocation size. One interesting feature of the reform of the textile allocation system is the press coverage that it received. While the rationalization plan may have already been in the minds of policy makers, the pressure from public debate probably had a strong influence. Encouraged by the success of the Spinners Association in obtaining the removal of the cotton import monopoly, the garment producers formed a new association in defiance of the Textile Producers Association. It was this newly formed association that lobbied for changes directly to the Ministry of Trade and indirectly by building up public support through the media.

The December 1987 package. In December 1987 measures to reform capital markets were announced. Deregulation of the capital market was aimed at reducing government intervention in the operations of the stock exchange and at introducing over-the-counter trading. Foreigners were allowed to purchase stocks in Indonesian capital markets.

Other important deregulations were simplification of licenses for hotels; treatment of joint ventures as domestic companies if 51 percent of equity is Indonesian or if 20 percent of stock is sold through capital markets; defining exporters as firms that export 65 percent or more of production; and elimination of export licenses, except for quota items.

During the period from December 1987 to October 1988 investors were not certain of the direction of deregulation, and there was much speculation about further deregulation. At the same time there was an increased use of export bans on raw and semiprocessed products, which ran counter to the moves to deregulate.

Substantive reforms and a clearer direction. After a lull of eight months, several major deregulation packages were announced beginning in October 1988. The first was the long awaited package to deregulate the financial sector. The main aim of the package was to increase competition between banks, thus increasing efficiency and reducing intermediation costs. Eventually it would reduce interest rates and increase the availability of investment funds, which are crucial for future growth of the economy.

The deregulation measures included removing restrictions that limited the number of banks. New domestic banks would be allowed, foreign banks could enter Indonesia as joint ventures (up to 85 percent equity), and geographical and product restrictions faced by existing foreign banks were removed. State enterprises were allowed to place deposits in nonstate banks.

In order to remove the bias against investment in capital markets and move toward a consistent tax system, the tax exemption of interest on deposits was removed. To offset the resulting increase in the cost of funds, the reserve requirements for banks were lowered from 15 percent to 2 percent.

The second deregulation package, in November 1988, related to shipping, distribution of goods by foreign investors, and nontariff barriers. Regulations on routes and licensing of interisland shipping were removed, and the requirement to use domestically produced ships was relaxed. Foreign investors were allowed to distribute their own goods by setting up a joint venture company. Finally, further changes from nontariff barriers to tariff barriers were initiated in the two most important areas, raw materials for plastics and steel products. One feature that emerged around this time was that the government began announcing planned deregulation packages. It was announced that three more deregulation packages in investment, capital markets, and state enterprises would follow.

In accordance with the announcement, the third package, announced on 20 December 1988, was a package to deregulate capital markets and financial services. The main components allowed the opening of a private stock exchange, the opening of stock exchanges in cities other than Jakarta, and improvement of securities transactions at the Jakarta Stock Exchange. Nonexistent or unclear regulations in several financial services such as hire-purchase, venture capital, leasing, brokerage, credit cards, and consumer credit were rationalized and clarified. The final component was the long awaited deregulation of the insurance industry: new entry was allowed and various restrictions were removed.

In mid-1989 the two packages on investment and state enterprises followed. The investment priority list of the Board of Investment was replaced by a shorter negative list indicating which sectors were closed for investment. Although there are still some criticisms regarding the lack of clarity in the selection criteria of sectors in the negative list, the system is an improvement over the more cumbersome priority list. The deregulation on state enterprises is not yet substantive; the main change announced is that state enterprises are now allowed to sell up to 20 percent of their shares to the public.

Conclusions

Two main conclusions can be drawn from this study of Indonesian policy reforms, especially in the post-petroleum-boom period. First is the importance of sequencing policies. Trade and industry reforms cannot be analyzed in a vacuum since it is increasingly recognized that the design and implementation of trade policy is a complex task and is related to other overlapping policy instruments and objectives. "Since it is not feasible or even desirable to undertake all reforms simultaneously, the coordination and phasing of policy reforms becomes one of the central issues in implementing trade liberalization" (Bhattacharya and Linn 1988:61).

The Indonesian government has responded to economic crises by undertaking appropriate economic-stabilization policies, notably with respect to exchange-rate adjustments, reduction of the fiscal deficit, and consistent monetary policy. Macroeconomic stabilization was followed by resource-mobilization policies.

The 1983 devaluation came before budget cuts, banking deregulation, and tax reforms. The 1986 devaluation was followed by further banking and financial sector deregulation and increased efforts to collect taxes. After introducing resource-mobilization policies, the government adopted policies to reduce costs or increase efficiency. These policies combined a simplification of administrative procedures with rationalization of incentives. The sequence has been reform in trade policies first and then reforms in industrial or investment policies. The government has shown a willingness to undertake drastic reforms, such as the customs cleanup, and this has an important psychological effect. After reforms in the trade and industrial sectors, reforms followed in other areas such as transportation and domestic regulations.

The sequencing evident in reforms indicates that initial conditions of macroeconomic stability and appropriate real exchange-rate management are important precursors to more substantive, and potentially more un-popular, trade and industry reforms. The preannouncement of the direction of deregulation, which has recently been introduced, is also an important feature in the planning of sequencing.

The second conclusion is the importance of a stable core group of policy makers who work closely as a team. The main thrust of policy making must be attributed to them. That trade deregulation did not follow the 1983 devaluation could be explained by the fact that the consensus, probably even among the technocrat group, was still heavily biased toward import substitution.

There has been much debate about the desirability of policy input from multilateral agencies and foreign consultants. Although both the World Bank and International Monetary Fund provide input (in recent times conditionality on new loans has become stronger), the core group remains composed of experienced policy makers able to select the policy input desired. Now there is also a lot of common ground in policy orientation, which has facilitated the realization of the deregulation packages.

The main motivations for using foreign consultants as a source of policy input or packaging for policies are a desire for confidentiality and a lack of domestic consultants. Indigenous abilities in this area could be developed by building up the capabilities of research departments in ministries and centralizing some domestic experts in an ongoing policy research body like the Korea Development Institute. There are many well-trained and capable people whose potential remains untapped because of poor management, lack of incentives (both financial and work environment), and lack of coordination.

There are two ways to achieve better local capability in policy input. The quickest is to enforce transfer of technology from foreign consultants to domestic consultants by making the latter equal counterparts. This has not always worked in the past due to mismatching and lack of continuous effort. The other way is through education and training as well as providing an appropriate degree of autonomy and incentives to domestic experts.

Appendix

Structure of Ministries

National Planning Agency (BAPPENAS)
State minister/chairman
Junior minister/vice chairman
Deputies:
  Economics
  Social and cultural
  Fiscal and monetary affairs
  • trade
  • foreign economic cooperation
  • budget and monetary affairs
  • regional/multilateral issues and balance of payments
  • economic analyses and statistics
  • quantitative studies and macro planning
  Monitoring and planning
  Manpower and natural resource development
  Administration

Ministry of Finance
Minister
Junior minister
Directorate generals:
  Budgetary affairs
  Customs
  Tax
  Monetary affairs (domestic and international)
  Budget, credit, and state finance
  Analysis

Ministry of Trade
Minister
Junior minister
Directorate generals:
  Domestic trade
  • agriculture and forest products distribution
  • mining and industrial products
  • development of trading activities
  • development of trading facilities
  • meteorology

Foreign trade
  • exports of mining and industrial products
  • exports of agriculture and forestry products
  • imports
  • foreign trade relations
  • standardization
  • normalization and quality control
Directorate general level agencies:
  National Agency for Export Development
    Center for Research and Development
      • head, research of domestic trade
      • head, foreign trade research and development
    Agency for Commodity Exchange

Ministry of Industry
Minister
Junior minister
Directorate generals:
  Basic metals and machinery industry
  Basic chemicals
  Multifarious industries
Directorate general level agencies:
  Industrial and Research Development Agency
    • industry research center
    • R&D for industrial infrastructure
    • development of investment climate
    • industrial promotion and exhibition center
  Education and Training Center

Coordinating Ministry for Economic, Financial and Industrial Affairs and Development
Coordinating minister
Assistants to coordinating ministers:
  Monetary affairs, balance of payments, and public finance
  International relations
  Agriculture and population
  Industry, mines, and energy
  Facilities and services

FINANCIAL LIBERALIZATION IN AUSTRALIA AND NEW ZEALAND

Like many developing countries, Australia and New Zealand have been commodity exporters subject to big swings in their current-account balances. Like many Asian countries, Australia and New Zealand are realizing the importance of diversifying their economies by improving the efficiency of other sectors so as to create opportunities for expanding exports and for more broadly based growth. Although there is a long way to go, restructuring is occurring in hitherto sheltered areas in manufacturing; in the services sector including, for example, education; and even in the labor market.

In Australia these reforms were preceded by liberalization of the financial market, which was virtually in place by the time the Hawke-Keating Labor government committed itself to substantial restructuring of other sectors. Financial liberalization in New Zealand was conceived as part of a comprehensive economic policy-reform package. In both countries, however, financial liberalization proceeded at a rapid pace and without any apparent serious opposition from interested parties.

Australian financial deregulation began gathering momentum in 1979 with the appointment, by the Liberal-National party coalition government, of the Committee of Inquiry into the Australian Financial System (the Campbell Committee). This committee provided a forum for interest groups (including the Treasury, the Reserve Bank, the Bankers' Association, the Bank Employees' Union, and academics writing commissioned studies) to consider seriously the issue of financial deregulation and to air their views. The committee recommended substantial deregulation. Perhaps as a result of the process of written and oral submissions, (covered heavily in the press) and the publication of the committee's *Interim Report* (Australia 1980), the government of the day moved to remove interest-rate ceilings on bank deposits in December 1980, before the *Final Report* (Australia 1981) was published in 1981. By 1982 quantitative bank lending guidance ceased, portfolio controls on savings banks were relaxed, and a market-oriented, interest-rate-sensitive system (the tender system) for selling government securities was introduced. The Labor government, which took office in March 1983, set up the Martin Review Group to review the recommendations of the Campbell Committee. The Martin review took the economic arguments for deregulation provided by the Campbell Report and developed the blueprint for continued deregulation under a traditionally interventionist Labor government. The remaining major deregulatory steps were subsequently accomplished. These included the abolition of exchange controls and the floating of the Australian dollar in December 1983, as well as the entry of forty new foreign-exchange dealers in 1984 and of sixteen foreign banks by February 1985. The most recent major step was the abolition in August 1988 of the statutory reserve deposit requirement of trading banks (commercial banks). These steps, as well as New Zealand's, are chronicled in the appendixes to this chapter.

Although it has been claimed that part of the reform program (notably on the trade side) had begun before the New Zealand Labor government came into office in July 1984 (Blyth 1987), the pace of financial deregulation since that date has been rapid. Interest-rate controls on financial institutions were removed during July and August 1984, exchange controls were removed in December 1984, and the New Zealand dollar was floated by March 1985. All compulsory ratios imposed on financial institutions (including the reserve asset ratio) were abolished in February 1985, and a policy admitting new banks was announced in November 1985. By March 1988, ten new banks had been registered.

It has been argued that in the 1970s accelerating inflation and technological innovations combined to reduce the effectiveness of banking regulations in Western economies (Kane 1981). Accelerating inflation increased the effective cost of interest-rate ceilings to banks. At the same time, technological advances epitomized in the information revolution made it possible to provide close substitutes for the products and services that were under regulation. Therefore, from the banks' point of view, the costs of regulation had risen while the costs of evading the regulations had fallen. Incentives for widespread evasion emerged, and deregulation was in the banks' interest.

At the same time, high and variable rates of inflation made savers more conscious of interest-rate differentials and led deposits away from the regulated institutions (banks) toward nonbank financial intermediaries. Improvements in information technology also enabled the nonbank financial intermediaries to offer close substitutes for the products and services offered by banks. These factors underpinned the accelerating growth of nonbank financial intermediaries in the 1970s and intensified the process of financial disintermediation. This process reduced the effectiveness of regulation as a form of monetary control and encouraged the adoption of more market-oriented strategies by the central banks. This argument made it clear that deregulation was in the public interest. The coincidence of public and private interests constituted a major factor in the success of financial liberalization (Harper 1986).

If indeed it were accepted that the financial sector was more amenable to rapid deregulation in the 1980s than other sectors of the economy, then the literature on sequencing of liberalization loses much of its practical significance. Rapid financial liberalization accompanied by contractionary monetary policy would result in increases in domestic interest rates and hence in appreciation of the nominal exchange rate. Rigidities in the labor and goods market would translate this into an appreciation of the real exchange rate. It is argued that the resulting difficulties experienced by the export sector would put pressure on other sectors to liberalize (Buckle 1987, Spencer and Carey 1988). On the other hand, this "hard landing" scenario could jeopardize the rest of the reform program.

The process of financial growth and financial reintermediation seems to be common to both countries, as are the challenges confronting the monetary authorities in redefining monetary aggregates and reinterpreting their relationships with policy instruments and their impact on income and inflation. Furthermore, increased competition in the financial sector carries with it greater risks of default and bankruptcies. The task of setting prudential guidelines without simultaneously impeding competition and reducing incentives for prudence by the financial institutions themselves proved to be another major challenge for governments in the late 1980s.

This chapter first attempts to explain why financial liberalization took place in Australia and New Zealand. The second section contrasts New Zealand's current situation with Australia's experience with government action in the foreign exchange and labor markets. The third section discusses the experiences of the two countries in a financially deregulated environment.

Why Financial Liberalization in Australia and New Zealand?

Neither Australia nor New Zealand has a tradition of strong commitment to the ideology of free markets. The desire for government involvement in most spheres of life has been traced back to the nineteenth century in New Zealand (Sinclair 1980) and to the convict heritage in Australia (Sanders 1988). The specific regulation of banks, however, stemmed from public sentiments during the depression of the 1930s (Reserve Bank of Australia November 1985, Blyth 1987). Legislation passed after World War II empowered governments to restrict entry into the banking industry, to call trading bank funds into statutory reserve deposits, to control the level and direction of trading and savings bank lending, to control interest rates, and to control foreign exchange and payments to and from foreign countries.[1] In addition, banks were required to keep certain proportions of their depositors' funds in government securities, and these controls in lesser degree were later extended to some nonbank financial intermediaries such as short-term money market dealers and life insurance companies. In the case of Australian life insurance companies, tax incentives were also used to promote the holding of government securities. From the banks' own point of view, the interest-rate ceilings on loans and ratio controls, including the statutory reserve assets ratio, constituted an implicit tax, in exchange for which they received rent from a legalized cartel formed through restricted entry. Interest-rate ceilings on deposits, on the other hand, were an implicit tax on the banks' depositors. When, as discussed below, developments in the 1970s substantially increased the cost of these implicit taxes, Australian bankers argued strongly for the rapid removal of direct controls, but were very much on the side of gradualism as far as the entry of new banks was concerned (Australian Bankers' Association 1979). Interestingly, there was no strong pressure from the New Zealand banks to abolish direct controls. This could reflect the fact that statutory reserve deposits in Australia paid only nominal interest rates (an increase from 0.75 percent to just over 2 percent between 1970 and 1976), whereas the required reserves in New Zealand had interest rates that generally followed the inflation rate, albeit with long lags.

Other interested parties believed that they benefited from regulations that channeled cheap bank funds to them, notably the housing industry, rural industries, and state government instrumentalities. Again, developments in the 1970s considerably weakened these benefits.

From a public policy or public interest point of view, governments saw financial regulations as a means of directing credit toward activities that Australian and New Zealand people deemed to be important. These included the provision of housing, the services provided by state governments, and farming. The regulations were also thought to facilitate monetary control while domestic interest rates were kept relatively low and stable. In this way, it was thought that investment and high levels of employment and income could be maintained without running the risk of inflation. Exchange controls, on the other hand, were applied to mobilize foreign-exchange earnings under the control of the central banks to ensure that they were employed for what were seen as priority purposes. In addition, by isolating domestic capital markets from world capital markets, exchange controls were intended to give the central banks greater control over money supply under the fixed (and later a crawling peg) exchange-rate regime. Furthermore, public interest was thought to be served by using regulations as a form of prudential control over banks and, to a lesser degree, over other custodians of the community's savings.

Developments in the 1970s common to both countries, namely accelerating inflation, large government budget deficits, and advances in information technology and financial innovation, drastically changed the above equations (Kane 1981, Keeler 1984, Harper 1986).

Inflation. In the 1970s, the average annual inflation rates for Australia and New Zealand were 10.5 percent and 12.5 percent respectively, compared with the Organization for Economic Cooperation and Development (OECD) average of 9.04 percent (OECD 1987). Nominal interest rates needed to rise in times of high inflation to maintain real rates of return to lenders. Statutory reserve deposits reduced profitability to trading banks, while interest-rate ceilings on deposits channeled depositors' funds away from banks toward nonbank financial intermediaries. The latter trend, which began in the 1950s, was intensified in part by the fact that inflation heightened the awareness of the household sector (the chief source of domestic savings in financial forms) to differential rates of return on their investments (Harper 1986) and reduced customer loyalty to banks (Reserve Bank of Australia February 1986). Table 8.1 shows the gap between controlled interest rates and market rates in Australia. The ninety-day bank bill rate is a market rate, and the trading bank maximum deposit rate for three- to six-month deposits is a regulated rate. Although the rates quoted in this table are perhaps more applicable to the corporate than to the household sector, they are indicative of interest rates generally.

Table 8.1 also shows that, in times of high inflation, interest rates on government securities were below market rates. This meant that the ratio controls requiring banks to hold, among other liquid assets, significant amounts of government securities became increasingly onerous as a form of implicit tax. Banks were again at a disadvantage when compared with other financial institutions with lower or negligible ratio controls.

Because of the uncertainties regarding real rates of return on investments, inflation also made investors less willing to hold long-term

TABLE 8.1   Interest Rates in Australia, 1970–1987 (percentage per year)

June	Trading banks' maximum fixed deposit rate	90-day bank bill rate	13-week Treasury notes, issue yields
1970	4.80	8.70	5.41
1971	5.00	8.15	5.37
1972	4.30	5.75	4.50
1973	4.30	6.40	4.91
1974	6.75	18.80	10.75
1975	9.00	8.80	7.81
1976	8.25	10.45	6.98
1977	8.25	11.10	8.60
1978	7.75	10.80	8.35
1979	7.75	10.35	9.02
1980	8.50	13.85	10.84
1981	12.25	16.00	13.31
1982	15.25	18.75	15.47
1983	13.20	13.60	11.93
1984	12.50	12.80	11.24
1985	discontinued	16.50	14.02
1986		14.80	12.38
1987		13.35	12.23

SOURCE: Reserve Bank of Australia, *Bulletin* database.

securities. Maturity controls over trading bank deposits made those institutions less able to cater to changing consumer tastes. It was therefore not surprising that, as Table 8.2 shows, the share of bank assets in Australia as a proportion of total assets in the financial sector (excluding the reserve bank) fell by 10 percentage points between 1967 and 1983. It started rising again only after the bulk of the deregulation was in place. The temporary recovery between 1973 and 1976 was attributed to the removal of interest-rate controls on trading banks' certificates of deposit in September 1973. The loss of market share on the part of the savings banks to the nonbank savings institutions is more dramatically illustrated in Figure 8.1, which shows the assets held by savings banks, credit unions, and building societies as a proportion of total assets of these three groups.

Table 8.2 also shows the share of trading bank assets as a proportion of private sector credit in New Zealand. Although the general declining trend is similar to that of Australia, the New Zealand picture is complicated by the fact that interest-rate ceilings on banks were removed in 1976, but were reimposed in 1981. Hence, there was some regaining of market share by New Zealand banks, back to 60 percent in 1977, before falling to a low 53 percent in 1984, just before interest-rate controls were

TABLE 8.2	Market Share of Banks in Australia and New Zealand, 1967–1986 (percentage)	
	Assets of trading and savings banks as a percentage of total financial sector assets (excluding reserve bank), Australia	Claims of trading banks as a percentage of private sector credit, New Zealand
1967	49.4	62.8
1968	48.6	61.4
1969	47.2	62.2
1970	45.1	62.0
1971	43.7	61.4
1972	41.5	59.2
1973	42.4	60.3
1974	42.7	59.3
1975	44.2	60.7
1976	44.5	58.7
1977	43.2	60.0
1978	42.0	57.1
1979	51.5	56.6
1980	41.2	55.5
1981	40.6	54.4
1982	39.8	56.3
1983	39.3	53.9
1984	40.4	53.3
1985	41.0	54.7
1986	42.3	55.5

SOURCES: Reserve Bank of Australia, *Bulletin, Financial Flow Accounts Supplement*, various years; communications with Reserve Bank of New Zealand.

again lifted. This difference in historical experience, together with the differential interest rates paid on required reserve deposits, could explain the more aggressive attitude in favor of deregulation on the part of the Australian banks that was not present in the New Zealand banks. At the same time, the New Zealand banks did not oppose deregulation.

Accelerating inflation also posed difficulties for both governments. By requiring banks to hold large portions of their assets in government securities that had been rendered illiquid and low yielding by inflation, the regulations were in fact acting against prudential considerations. In addition, sufficient funds were not being channeled into the desired sectors as originally intended. The declining share of bank assets shown in Table 8.2 meant that, although the proportion of bank lending to favored sectors might have been higher with regulations than without, the level of lending might have been the same or even lower (Spencer and Carey 1988). Furthermore, as noted in the Campbell Report (Australia 1981), in

---

FIGURE 8.1   Assets of Australian Savings Banks, Credit Unions, and Building Societies as a Percentage of Their Total Assets, 1964–1986

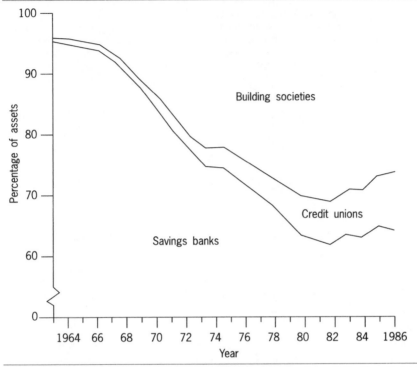

SOURCE: Reserve Bank of Austraila, *Statistical Bulletin: Financial Flow Accounts Supplement*, June 1981 and July 1987.

---

situations of credit rationing, banks would favor borrowers with lower risks—larger borrowers with either collateral or a previous record of doing business with the bank. This is a familiar observation, common to many countries that have financial repression.

One of the factors that led the Australian Liberal-National coalition government to review the financial system was a concern about the shortage of funds for small businesses. This was consistent with the effect of credit rationing in existence at the time (Harper 1986). Small borrowers, in housing finance for example, had to turn to higher-cost funds, such as solicitors' funds (Australia 1981, Spencer and Carey 1988). The move away from large financial intermediaries toward direct financing (that is, the process of financial disintermediation) was very much a trend observed in the 1970s and entailed high "efficiency costs," particularly in the case of small lenders and borrowers. The size of this cost could be gauged by the fact that reintermediation from direct financing back to banks is a significant trend in deregulated Australia and that interest-rate margins of banks have significantly narrowed in Australia since the early 1980s, reflecting increased competition (Beetham 1987).

Finally, high inflation meant that the central banks in both countries needed effective monetary policies. Direct controls on banks no longer provided the capacity to apply sustained and independent pressure on domestic monetary conditions because of the process of financial disintermediation described above. The regulations themselves had encouraged the growth of fringe institutions outside the regulatory net (Reserve Bank of New Zealand April 1985). Greater reliance therefore had to be placed on market-oriented strategies, such as open-market sales of government securities by the central banks. Open-market sales reduce the price and increase the yields on government securities, and hence result in more general increases in domestic interest rates than direct controls on the banking system alone.

Significant increases in domestic interest rates would, however, engender inflows of foreign capital. Under the pegged exchange-rate regimes existing in Australia and New Zealand before financial liberalization, capital inflows increased the central banks' international reserves and money base, thereby offsetting part of the tight money policy. Exchange controls (which included controls over inflows for part of the 1970s in Australia) were intended to prevent this from happening, but by the late 1970s financial innovations were eroding the effectiveness of these in Australia. Estimates of the offset coefficient for Australia before 1976 averaged about negative 0.5 (Porter 1974, Murray 1978).[2] Studies for the period after 1976, however, indicated a much closer degree of integration with world financial markets (Polasek and Lewis 1985).

In order to regain effective control over domestic monetary conditions under these circumstances, the central banks would have needed to re-establish effective control over foreign-exchange flows or float their currencies. To have an effective float, however, exchange controls would have to be abolished.

At the time of their submissions to the Campbell Committee, both the Australian Treasury (1981) and the Reserve Bank of Australia (1979) were reluctant to adopt a flexible exchange-rate regime. The Treasury sought to use an overvalued Australian dollar to fight inflation by lowering the level of activity in the economy and depressing the price of imports in the consumer price index. In addition, given the rigidities that existed in the Australian labor market at the time, there were fears that a float would initially lead to depreciation of the Australian dollar and increases in domestic prices which, through wage indexation, would feed into wage increases. The resulting loss in Australia's international competitiveness would lead to further depreciation and wage-price increases in a self-perpetuating spiral (Obstfeld 1983, Whitelaw 1986, private communication).

By 1983 the ineffectiveness of exchange controls in preventing integration with world financial markets was made apparent by two bouts of speculative flows across the exchange: The first was a speculative outflow before the election in March 1983, which resulted in a 10 percent devaluation. The second was a speculative inflow in December 1983 in anticipation of a revaluation. It was inflation, together with technological advances and financial innovations integrating the Australian market with international capital markets, that forced the decision to liberalize the foreign-exchange market.

Even though there does not appear to be similar evidence that financial innovation in New Zealand significantly eroded the effectiveness of capital controls, their success in impeding foreign-exchange flows is highly questionable (Carey and Duggan 1986). In June and July 1984, before the 20 percent devaluation, substantial outflows occurred even within the current account.[3] As in Australia, the need to have an effective anti-inflationary monetary policy was an important reason for floating the New Zealand dollar. Even more so than in Australia, however, inflation and interest-rate ceilings had so reduced real interest rates that domestic savings were seriously discouraged. Added to this, exchange controls, to the extent that they were effective, prevented New Zealanders from taking advantage of higher real rates of return elsewhere in the world, a process that would have put upward pressure on nominal interest rates in New Zealand (Spencer and Carey 1988). Domestic investments were artificially encouraged, particularly in real assets for which inflation had resulted in nontaxable capital gains (for example, in commercial buildings). Removing interest-rate and foreign-exchange controls was seen to be an important step in rectifying the serious misallocation of resources brought on by, among other things, accelerating inflation.

Increased government borrowing. Substantially larger government deficits were also common to both countries in the late 1970s. Government deficits as a proportion of Australian gross domestic product (GDP) rose from an average of 1.2 percent per year in the first half of the 1970s to an average of 3.8 percent in the second half of the 1970s. Comparable figures for New Zealand were 2.3 percent and 6.7 percent respectively. Large government expenditures coupled with an unwillingness to increase taxes meant that the deficits had to be financed by borrowing. Public sector borrowing requirements in Australia averaged 4.7 percent of GDP in the second half of the 1970s, and rose to almost 7 percent of GDP by 1983–1984. The larger presence of governments in the financial markets further eroded the market shares of banks, beyond that caused by nonbank financial intermediaries. It is generally recognized, for instance, that the Australian savings bonds introduced by the government in 1976, and paying attractive rates of interest, absorbed a large share of savings that had traditionally gone to banks (Carew 1985). Likewise, the high-yielding inflation adjusted bonds, as well as the first Kiwi savings stock introduced in 1983, in New Zealand attracted very large volumes of savings away from domestic financial institutions.

Substantial increases in government borrowing necessitated a more market-oriented sales program for government securities, including more market-oriented interest rates. In the early 1980s the tender system for selling government securities replaced the "tap" system in both Australia and New Zealand. In theory, the tender system enabled the authorities to determine the quantities of government securities to be offered, while the market (the bidders) determined the interest rates on these securities. The authorities could therefore be more confident that the securities on offer would be bought. In contrast, the earlier tap system required the authorities to determine the interest rates on the securities, and the market then determined the amount to be purchased. In practice, when yields on government securities were below market during much of the 1970s, the institutions buying government securities were predominantly the captive ones, those required to hold certain proportions of their assets in that form. As growth in these institutions stagnated because of the increased costs of the tax implied by the regulations, the sale of government securities likewise stagnated (one exception to stagnating growth in that period was life insurance companies in Australia).

The efficient working of the tender system was frustrated by the existence of interest-rate ceilings on government securities. For example, in New Zealand between September 1983 (when the tender system was introduced) and July 1984 (when the government was willing to accept market interest rates on its securities), it was clear from the bids accepted that the government was not willing to pay more than 11 percent on conventional bonds and 6 percent on index-linked bonds. Consequently, subscription ratios were, on several occasions, insufficient to cover even two-thirds of the tenders. In contrast, the tenders offered after July 1984 had subscription ratios three to four times greater than the amount on offer (Reserve Bank of New Zealand August 1985). Hence, large government borrowing requirements necessitated a market-oriented system for selling government securities, namely a tender system without interest-rate ceilings. Once government securities were paying market interest rates, however, the ratio controls became redundant, as institutions would then hold those securities willingly as part of their portfolio.

It is clear therefore that in both Australia and New Zealand large public sector borrowing requirements in the late 1970s and early 1980s were an important force behind removal of interest-rate ceilings and deregulation of ratio controls on financial institutions.

Advances in information technology. It has been pointed out that financial intermediation is an information-intensive industry, so that the information revolution in the 1970s substantially changed the cost structure of the industry (Harper 1986). In Australia Swan and Harper (1982) argued that the relative lack of union pressure in the nonbank financial intermediaries, as well as the more competitive environment in which these institutions operated, led them to adopt labor-saving technologies ahead of the banks. In addition to the factors discussed above, this step further enhanced the competitiveness of the nonbanks with the banks.

Technological advances also enhanced financial innovation by increasing the variety of financial instruments available and by reducing the costs of their introduction into the marketplace. Some of these new instruments hurt the banks by enabling nonbanks to provide close substitutes for the services offered by banks, thereby reducing their market share. Financial innovation also enabled banks to circumvent regulations. Some examples of close substitutes to products offered by banks are telephone bill paying and automatic fund transfer facilities offered by building societies and credit unions in lieu of checking accounts offered exclusively by banks. Another example is the mutual indemnity contract in Australia, which led to the growth of currency hedging facilities offered by brokers and merchant banks in competition with official hedging facilities handled by the trading banks.

It was the growth of the private currency hedge market that underpinned the final decision to liberalize the foreign-exchange market in Australia (Polasek and Lewis 1985). This development vividly illustrates the argument that financial innovation in the market eventually led to deregulation in the same market.

To prevent private capital flows from nullifying the effects of monetary policy in Australia under a fixed, and later crawling peg, exchange-rate regime, many private capital transactions were discouraged. The regulatory framework sought to separate trade transactions from capital transactions. One development was the official hedge market, where the reserve bank set the forward rate and stood by as dealer-of-last-resort, while the four major trading banks were given exclusive authority in foreign-exchange dealings and acted as agents for the reserve bank in evaluating each transaction involving foreign exchange, including forward foreign-exchange cover. Legitimate trading transactions were permitted cover, while most capital transactions were not given cover. The generalized float after 1973 increased the magnitude of exchange risks for the reserve bank in its role as dealer-of-last-resort, and in an effort to limit its exposure to exchange risks, the reserve bank further restricted the eligibility criteria for official forward cover so that even some trade transactions could not be covered.

This spurred the development of the mutual indemnity contract whereby the parties (exporters, importers, borrowers, and lenders) agreed to indemnify one another against capital losses brought about by exchange-rate fluctuations. The contracts were to be settled in Australian dollars so that they escaped exchange controls. The contracts were open to capital as well as trade transactions. Merchant banks initially acted as brokers, but soon entered the market as principals. This move greatly enhanced the growth of the private currency hedge market. All transactions, current and capital, could then be summed and settled in Australian dollars. Only when actual funds had to be transferred out of Australia would exchange-control regulations apply. At that point, it was not difficult to disguise capital transactions so that in practice, the new financial instrument (namely, the indemnity contract) circumvented exchange control regulations regarding private capital flows.

Official sanction was given to the private currency hedge market in 1975, and the merchant banks in that market were so successful and provided such competition for the banks that by 1979 the Australian government had to permit the trading banks to conduct their own inter-bank hedge market.

More important, the private currency hedge market provided a channel through which private capital flows could occur and be covered forward. Demand for foreign borrowings came in the early 1980s during the resources boom in Australia. The subsequent build-up of large amounts of foreign debt formed a pool of potentially volatile funds (aided no doubt by international funds transfer facilities) that provided the basis for the massive speculations in 1983 that led to the aforementioned float and abolition of exchange control regulations.

This episode clearly demonstrates the point made by the governor of the Reserve Bank of Australia that deregulation "is a deliberate step: it is an official recognition or sanction of change" (Reserve Bank of Australia February 1986). It is undeniable that change had been occurring in the financial markets of Australia and New Zealand as a result of common developments in the 1970s—namely accelerating inflation, large government budget deficits, advances in information technology, and financial innovations. In turn, change in the financial markets brought about a confluence of public and private forces in favor of liberalization (Harper 1986).

Public interest and private interest. It has been argued so far that by the 1980s—from the point of view of macroeconomic management, prudential considerations, efficient allocation of resources, and redistribution—a good argument existed for deregulation in the Australian and New Zealand financial and foreign-exchange markets. In short, a convincing case existed for liberalization in the public interest.

At the same time, the increasing loss of market share by the banks, which was a result of regulation, formed a private interest argument for deregulation. Nonbank financial intermediaries were interested in opportunities to operate in sections of the market denied to them by regulations—foreign-exchange dealings and checking account facilities for example. In fact, merchant banks were given foreign-exchange dealerships in Australia in exchange for possible losses in market share resulting from deregulation of banks. Bank employee unions and farmers in both Australia and New Zealand were prepared to trade the advantages of a protected environment for the prospects of more employment from new banks in the first case (Harper 1986) and a lower value of the domestic dollar in the latter (Buckle 1987). Even the powerful home mortgage lobby in Australia was appeased by a series of gradual steps resulting in the fact that interest-rate ceilings on home loans valued below A$100,000 would not be removed retroactively from April 1986. Entry of foreign banks was sold to the labor caucus by the Australian treasurer on the argument that the oligopolistic powers of the domestic banks should be challenged by bringing in competition from overseas banks.

Governments were able to reconcile private interests in the case of financial liberalization because inflation, large public-sector borrowing, and financial innovation had already changed the way in which interest groups perceived the cost-benefit trade-off under regulation. The political climate in Australia and New Zealand was thus ripe for financial deregulation in the 1980s. Perhaps the main lesson to be learned is that liberalization is not a unilateral decision on the part of governments. For it to be successful, liberalization must be underpinned by economic developments in the private sector.

Exchange-Rate Overshooting and Sequencing of Liberalization

Experience in New Zealand. Ever since the 20 percent devaluation in July 1984 and the floating of the New Zealand dollar in March 1985, the real exchange rate has appreciated (see Figure 8.2).[4] As the real exchange rate expresses the relative prices of domestic and foreign goods measured in terms of foreign currency, the appreciation of New Zealand's real effective exchange rate means a deterioration in its international competitiveness. Figure 8.2 shows that by mid-1987 New Zealand had lost the competitiveness gained through the July 1984 devaluation and that the real exchange rate has been trending upward since then. Indeed, it has been argued (Buckle 1987) that the real exchange rate was prevented from trending upward between the September quarter 1985 and September quarter 1986 only by the easing of liquidity conditions, and hence domestic interest rates, during that period.

FIGURE 8.2   Real Effective Exchange Rate of New Zealand, 1980–1988

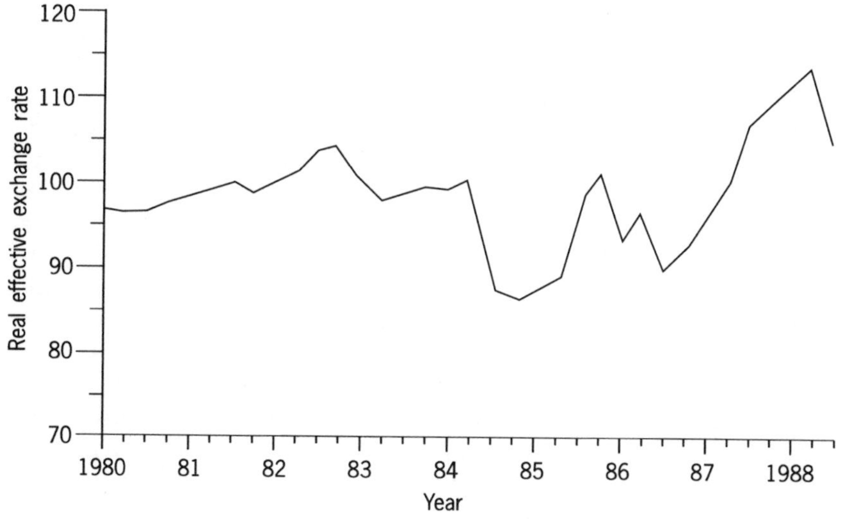

SOURCE: Reserve Bank of New Zealand.

The resulting squeeze on the export sector and on domestic activity in general has engendered fears that the entire liberalization process is being forced to slow down (*Australian Financial Review* 1988 a, b, c, d). Reports of union unrest and pressures from farmers and other exporters cannot be taken lightly. On the other hand, the success on the inflation front and the decline of the budget deficit have generated optimistic assessments that domestic interest rates and exchange rates will fall by 1989 (van Wyngen 1988).[5] In any case, it seems to be generally agreed that the currently high value of the New Zealand dollar does not reflect higher foreign investments because of improved productivity in New Zealand industries (Buckle 1987, Spencer and Carey 1988, van Wyngen 1988). Rather, capital inflows since liberalization of the financial and foreign-exchange markets have been almost entirely in portfolio investments responding to interest-rate differentials between New Zealand and abroad. In other words, real exchange rates have risen higher than are consistent with the long-run current-account balance.

Exchange-rate overshooting. The theory of exchange-rate overshooting is well established in the literature (Dornbusch 1976). In general, the theory is consistent with the argument that, in the short run, interest rates and exchange rates are determined by demand and supply of stocks of financial assets in the economy, rather than by real factors such as productivity growth. Hence, nominal exchange rates can be quite volatile in the short run, fluctuating around their long-run equilibrium levels. In the New Zealand case, liberalization of the financial and foreign-exchange markets, together with tight monetary policy, led to rapid increases in nominal interest rates—the treasury bill rate rose from about 14 percent at the beginning of 1986 to almost 25 percent before easing to 17 percent at the beginning of 1988. This greatly enhanced the attractiveness of financial assets denominated in New Zealand dollars, resulting in capital inflow and appreciation of the nominal exchange rate. If the lower prices of imports and overseas loan service resulting from such appreciation were to be fed through to the economy generally (perhaps via reductions in nominal wages and prices), then in theory, the real exchange rate need not appreciate. However, adjustments in the commodity and factor markets are much slower than in the assets market. Hence, the New Zealand price level would not have fallen while the New Zealand dollar had risen, making New Zealand exports uncompetitive in world markets. Therefore, a nominal disturbance (appreciation of the nominal exchange rate) results in real effects in the form of reduced exports and lower levels of economic activity.

Sequencing of liberalization. The phenomenon of real exchange-rate overshooting would presumably be heightened when the foreign-exchange market is deregulated while substantial rigidity exists in the goods and factor markets. This constitutes the basis for the recommendation that the foreign-exchange market should be liberalized only after commodity, factor, and financial markets have been liberalized (McKinnon 1982, Mathieson 1986). A related argument is that since investment decisions in financial assets can be reversed more quickly and with less cost than investments in real production, trade flows should be liberalized before international financial flows (Frenkel 1983). These arguments constitute a body of literature known as the sequencing of liberalization. It is based on the experiences of economic reforms in the Southern Cone countries—Argentina, Uruguay, and Chile—during the mid-1970s (McKinnon 1982, Edwards 1984, Krueger 1984).

It should be noted at this point that real exchange-rate overshooting is a short-term phenomenon, although no one can be precise about how short. Hence, the sequencing recommendations are ultimately judgments about the pressures that might arise during the restructuring process.

If such capital inflows are absorbed in real terms, this could force a trade deficit and real exchange-rate appreciation in the economy. The resulting (severe) antiprotection in the production of tradable goods then depresses the economy and impedes political momentum for eliminating import restrictions and export subsidies (McKinnon 1982, 163).

The implication is that, by carefully liberalizing the economy in a certain sequence, the government could bring about a softer landing than would otherwise be the case. A hard landing could result in political pressures that threaten to disrupt the rest of the reform.

In the context of New Zealand, real exchange-rate appreciation would have occurred even if New Zealand had stayed on the pegged exchange-rate regime. The absence of an effective anti-inflationary policy would have resulted in declines in New Zealand's international competitiveness, unless matched by very timely and well judged devaluations—a very difficult task, in reality. On the other hand, an effective anti-inflationary monetary policy in the context of a pegged exchange-rate regime would have required the authorities to extend the system of exchange controls by imposing controls on capital inflows and, judging by the experience of June and July 1984, control over current-account items as well. In addition, it might have been necessary to tighten surveillance, perhaps by removing the foreign-exchange dealerships from the merchant banks, and concentrating controls with the trading banks. The arguments in the first part of this chapter have shown this to be quite contrary to the political climate of the day. Besides, as the Australian episode has shown, the authorities would have had a hard time stemming the forces of financial innovation. Therefore, in the case of New Zealand, careful sequencing of liberalization efforts was probably an unattainable ideal.

Experience in Australia. As mentioned earlier, deregulation of Australian financial and foreign-exchange markets was virtually complete when the government committed itself to restructuring other sectors of the economy. Nevertheless, there was no substantial tightening of monetary policy at the time of the float, since inflationary pressures were being reduced because of wage moderation resulting partly from the wages pause and the Prices and Incomes Accord. "Strong upward pressures on interest rates at this stage of the recovery would not be favorable to activity or external trade" (Reserve Bank of Australia 1984).[6] As Figure 8.3 shows, the real effective exchange rate appreciated somewhat over the course of 1984, but there was no sign of overshooting. Similar losses in international competitiveness were evident before 1983, before the float, because of high differential rates of inflation between Australia and its trading partners.

On the contrary, the real effective exchange rate of the Australian dollar depreciated throughout 1985, reaching a low point by mid-1986. At the same time, Australia's current-account deficit grew to an all time high of 6.3 percent of GDP, stemming mainly from the collapse in commodity

FIGURE 8.3   Real Effective Exchange Rate of Australia, 1980–1988

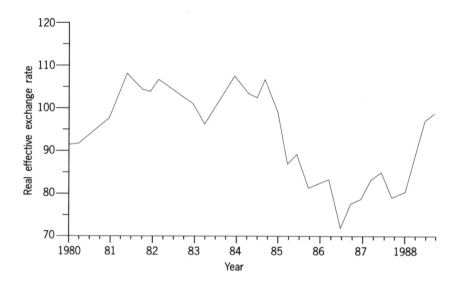

SOURCE: Morgan Guaranty, *World Financial Markets*.

prices. Fortunately, the Australian Treasury's fears of a depreciation-infla-
tion spiral did not materialize, perhaps as a result of the replacement of
direct nominal wage indexation by promises of tax cuts and superannuation benefits in the Prices and Incomes Accord. Real unit labor costs in
Australia fell by about 10 percent in the five years ending in 1988 (Australia, Treasury 1988). Hence, the depreciation of the nominal exchange
rate resulted in a depreciation of the real exchange rate and improvements
in Australia's competitive position internationally.

In addition, it appeared that the reserve bank intervened in February and April 1985, August 1986, and early 1987 to prevent what it
considered as unwarranted depreciation of the Australian dollar (Reserve Bank of Australia 1985, 1986, and 1987). In fact, the governor
specifically referred to intervention efforts to alleviate the problem of
overshooting (Reserve Bank of Australia September 1987). Furthermore,
there is econometric evidence (from a monthly estimation of a portfolio
balance model of the Australian financial sector since the float) that the
reserve bank intervened in the foreign-exchange market to steady the
real effective exchange rate, and that it sterilized about 48 percent of its
intervention efforts (Leung 1988).

Perhaps the difference in postfloat experience between New Zealand and Australia lies in the relatively greater flexibility in the Australian labor market. Whatever the criticisms of the accord (*Australian*

Financial Review 1988e), real wages in Australia have fallen in recent years. According to Corden (1988), Australian labor unions may have finally learned from the mistakes of the 1970s and early 1980s. Whether the severity of these lessons will tip the power balance between the unemployed and the employed so as to generate enough private interest support for deregulation of the labor market remains to be seen. As far as the financial markets were concerned, in the period 1983–1988, the accord seems to have resulted in less need (at least until recently) for severely contractionary monetary policies to bring inflation under control, thereby leaving greater scope for the Australian Reserve Bank to engage in sterilized interventions.

Challenges of a Deregulated Financial Environment

Better balance of macroeconomic policies. One of the main advantages of liberalization is that prices are allowed to become signals for allocation of resources in the economy. But as this chapter has already emphasized, financial prices such as exchange rates have a tendency to overshoot in the real world, which is full of rigidities in other markets. Given that careful sequencing may be impracticable, then the challenge for governments lies in a better balance of macroeconomic policies so that no undue pressure is placed on domestic interest rates leading to overshooting of exchange rates.

In Australia fiscal policy in the last five years has been restrictive and has taken some of the pressure off domestic interest rates. The total public-sector borrowing requirement has been reduced to zero compared with almost 7 percent of GDP in 1983–1984 (Australia, Treasury 1988). This reduction in borrowing, together with the Prices and Incomes Accord, contributed significantly to transforming the nominal exchange-rate depreciation of 1985–1986 into real depreciation (as shown in Figure 8.3), which in turn created opportunities for expansion of exports. At the same time employment has grown by 17 percent since 1983, and the unemployment rate has fallen from 10.5 percent to around 7 percent (Australia, Treasury 1988). The outcome has been a more receptive political climate for industrial restructuring and microeconomic reforms, the need for which was made apparent by the declining terms of trade and rapidly depreciating value of the Australian dollar in 1985–1986.

It does appear therefore that financial deregulation, removal of exchange controls, and floating of the Australian dollar in the first half of the 1980s required the Australian government to adopt a better balance of macroeconomic policies. In turn, this created an easier political climate for undertaking the microeconomic reforms in Australian industry assistance that should enable the country to attain higher long-term economic

TABLE 8.3   Exchange-Rate Volatility (April 1985–December 1987)

	Daily movements	Monthly movements
New Zealand dollar	1.04	3.96
Japanese yen	0.76	3.21
Australian dollar	0.86	2.94
United Kingdom pound sterling	0.89	2.51
Deutsche mark	0.88	2.58

NOTE: Standard deviations of first differences in logs of daily (monthly average) exchange rates, multiplied by 100; exchange rate measured against U.S. dollar.
SOURCE: Spencer and Carey 1988.

growth. The battle is far from over, however. The recent current-account deficits associated with appreciation in the real exchange rate back to the early 1985 levels (see Figure 8.3) could well be a sign of overshooting again. Perhaps excessive reliance is again being placed on monetary policy to curb economic activity and imports without sufficient regard to the relative price effects on trade of an above-equilibrium value of the Australian dollar. In addition, the implementation of microeconomic reforms may not have been sufficiently rapid to avoid supply constraints leading to overheating of the economy.

Fiscal, as well as monetary, restraint is also behind the New Zealand government's reform package. In spite of significant decreases in the budget deficit, the actual deficits still exceeded projections in the past three years (Wells 1987). This, together with insufficient flexibility in the labor market, could have contributed to the difficulties experienced by the export sector.

Volatility of exchange rates. In addition to the tendency for exchange rates to overshoot, another challenge posed by the liberalization of financial and foreign-exchange markets in Australia and New Zealand is the volatility of exchange rates. Floating currencies have, of course, shown much greater volatility than fixed exchange rates. The relative volatility of different currencies is also of interest. Table 8.3 compares the variability of the New Zealand and Australian dollar with other major currencies and shows that the New Zealand dollar, but not the Australian dollar, has been more volatile than the other major currencies.

At the same time, it should be recognized that under the pegged exchange-rate regime, the volatility inherent in the economy manifests itself in different ways. In particular, it shows up in domestic monetary conditions. Figure 8.4 shows cash rates (that is, the rate on overnight and call funds) for the three full months preceding the float in December 1983 and cash rates in the same three months two years after the float. The reduced volatility is quite remarkable. According to the reserve

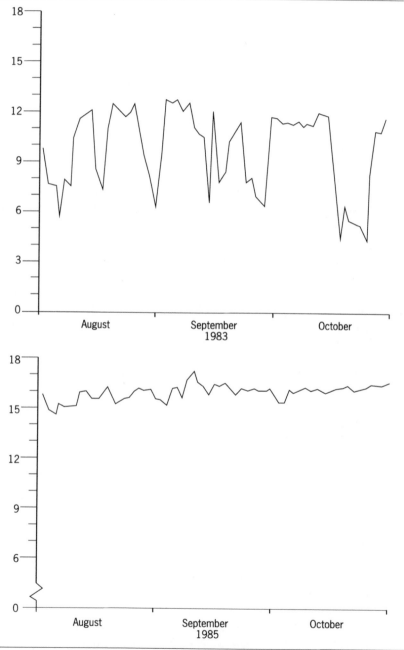

FIGURE 8.4   Australian Cash Interest Rates, August to October 1983 and August to October 1985

SOURCE: Reserve Bank of Australia, *Bulletin*, December 1986.

bank, "The standard deviation of the daily movement in the official cash rate was 2.64 percentage points in the two years before the float. In the three years since the float it has averaged 0.86 percent" (Reserve Bank of Australia December 1986).[7]

For the financial sector the challenge of exchange-rate volatility has been to develop instruments that will help participants in the foreign-exchange market handle the increased risks. A variety of instruments, including forward and futures markets, have been developed for this purpose.

Although there have been claims that the greater exchange-rate volatility has affected trade flows adversely, the evidence is not at all well established (IMF 1984, Spencer and Carey 1988).[8] Furthermore, the effect of greater volatility on margins charged in the New Zealand foreign-exchange market is unclear (Buckle 1987).

Financial growth, diversification, and reintermediation. An important objective of financial liberalization was to increase competition in the financial sector and the economy more generally. The introduction of sixteen new banks in Australia and ten new banks in New Zealand highlighted the process of competition in the financial sector. The existing banks in both countries have responded by diversifying from traditional areas of financial intermediation to other related types of financial services such as investment advice and financial planning, (including overseas investment advice), risk management, data processing, and information systems. This development is to be expected as the inputs consist largely of human capital and information—a combination that has significant economies of scale and can be applied with relative ease to related services (Harper and Karacaoglu 1987).

As a result both countries have seen financial reintermediation toward banks and away from fringe institutions since deregulation. As Table 8.2 indicates, in Australia the banks' share of total assets of the financial sector has been increasing since 1983. In Australia there is also some evidence indicating a shift away from direct financing toward intermediation (Reserve Bank of Australia October 1987). This should bring gains in efficiency through economies of scale.

The pressing need to acquire economies through diversification, together with the temporary shortage of skilled personnel and the efficiency gained through such personnel working as a team rather than as individuals, means that mergers and acquisitions would be the preferred arrangement for achieving diversification (Harper and Karacaoglu 1987). These have indeed been occurring in postliberalization Australia and New Zealand. Mergers among finance companies, stockbrokers, merchant banks, and building societies in New Zealand are documented by Harper and Karacaoglu (1987), and among Australian banks and stockbroking firms by Carew (1985). Although increased competition, rationalization, and diversification to take advantage of economies of scope would arguably lead to efficiency gains in the financial markets, the rapidly changing financial landscapes also bring new challenges for the monetary authorities. Some of the notable ones include prudential controls, the interpretation of monetary aggregates, and the transmission of monetary policy in a deregulated environment.

Prudential supervision. Rapid growth and increased competition leading to diversification and rationalization in the financial services industry raise the question of the viability of some of the financial intermediaries. As loss of confidence can spread very quickly in financial markets, the stability and integrity of the payments system (both domestic and international) clearly concern governments. There is no doubt that some degree of prudential supervision is necessary, but the difficulty lies in deciding whom to supervise, on the effect of such supervision on competition in the industry, and on how to supervise activities that are conducted increasingly in other countries (Reserve Bank of Australia February 1986).

The Reserve Bank of Australia has specific legislative responsibilities for protecting the depositors of banks. Hence a degree of supervisory power is exercised particularly in regard to the minimum capital ratio, which is higher for new banks than for existing trading banks. The argument is that until new banks establish their deposit base and their credibility in Australia, there is a need to ensure extra prudence.

The New Zealand Reserve Bank, on the other hand, does not include protection of bank depositors as part of its supervisory duties. It limits its role to the monitoring of all financial institutions and makes arrangements for the orderly exit of institutions that are no longer viable. What this would mean for depositors who could lose most or all their deposits remains to be seen.

Supervision of activities that are increasingly being conducted in foreign countries is being worked out in international forums—the Basel Concordat, for example. Judging by the rather different approaches toward prudential supervision between Australia and New Zealand, it may be quite difficult to secure international agreements on the supervision of activities that cross national borders.

What is money and how does monetary policy work? The removal of interest-rate controls and exchange controls, together with the floating of the currency, certainly gave the two reserve banks control over the money base. In this sense, deregulation has made the instruments of monetary policy much sharper, but this does not mean that the implementation of monetary policy is any easier. Both reserve banks have observed large increases in M3 since deregulation, and this could well have been the result of financial reintermediation toward the banking sector. Furthermore, market-determined interest rates and exchange rates can be strongly influenced by expectations of inflation or budget deficit outcomes for instance. Hence, not only has the composition of monetary aggregates and credit been changing as a result of deregulation, but the relationships between these aggregates and interest rates, exchange rates, income, and prices have become unclear.

It is not surprising that Stevens, Thorp, and Anderson (1987) found that several specifications of money demand equations for Australia using M3 were unstable when updated to include postderegulation data. In theory, money is defined as the only asset that is readily used in transactions and yet does not pay interest. This definition is fast becoming obsolete, and with it, our understanding of how monetary policy works.

As a result of these difficulties, from December 1984 conditional projection for M3 was suspended in Australia and was replaced by a continuous review of economic indicators in addition to the monetary aggregates—the so-called checklist. Similar difficulties are being experienced in New Zealand, and rigid targeting of any one particular financial variable is also being avoided (Spencer and Carey 1988).

In the meantime, the theoretical relationships between money and interest rates and the transmission of monetary policy in a deregulated world are topics of active current research in the central banks (see Blundell-Wignall and Thorp 1987, Morris 1988).

Conclusions

Financial liberalization in both Australia and New Zealand was rapid and far reaching. This chapter has argued that accelerating inflation, large government deficits, and financial innovation resulting from advances in information technology in the past decade created a political climate conducive to successful deregulation of the financial and foreign-exchange markets in the two countries. Research done within the reserve banks, treasuries, and academia has facilitated the process of deregulation. Likewise, skillful management enabled the implementation of the results of research.

This chapter has argued that liberalizing financial and foreign-exchange markets in sequence is neither practicable nor necessary. In Australia, financial deregulation required the government to adopt a better balance of fiscal and monetary policies, supported by some sort of incomes policy such as the Prices and Incomes Accord. This seemed to have engendered a smoother transition initially and generated a climate that was conducive to restructuring the other sectors of the economy. In spite of difficulties caused by exchange-rate overshooting, New Zealand's success in controlling inflation would mean that pressures on monetary policy and the New Zealand dollar could ease. Likewise, current experience in Australia's external balance will require the government to increase the momentum of microeconomic reforms and to maintain a consistent balance of macroeconomic policies.

In this way, financial liberalization is not only an official recognition of change that has been occurring in the financial sector, but is itself a catalyst generating further changes both in the financial sector and in the economy more generally.

Appendix 1

Chronology of Australian Financial Deregulation[9]

1979

January. Establishment of (Campbell) Committee of Inquiry into the Australian Financial System.

December. Introduction of tender system for Treasury note sales.

1980

December. Removal of interest-rate ceilings on deposits with trading and savings banks.

1981

February. Banking authority granted to Australian Bank Limited.

June. Treasurer authorizes mergers between Bank of New South Wales and Commercial Bank of Australia and between National Bank of Australia and Commercial Banking Company of Sydney.

August. Minimum maturity on trading bank certificates of deposit reduced from three months to thirty days.

November. Final Report of Campbell committee tabled.

1982

June. Cessation of quantitative bank lending guidance. Introduction of tender system for Treasury bond sales.

August. Relaxation of portfolio controls on savings banks.

1983

March. Australian Labor party elected to government.

May. Establishment of Martin Review Group.

December. Australian dollar floated; exchange controls abolished.

1984

February. Report of Martin Review Group tabled.

April. Deregulation of Australian stock exchanges.

June. Authority to trade in foreign exchange granted to forty nonbanks.

August. Removal of minimum and maximum maturities on trading and savings bank interest-bearing deposits. Savings banks permitted to offer checking facilities on all accounts.

September. "30/20" rule abolished.

1985

February. Sixteen foreign banks invited to establish operations in Australia.

April. Removal of remaining ceilings on bank loan interest rates, except ceiling on loans of less than A$100,000 for owner-occupied housing.

May. LGS (liquid assets plus government securities) convention replaced by prime assets ratio arrangements.

July. Treasury indexed bonds first issued.

October. Relaxation of foreign-investment policy relating to nonbank financial intermediaries.

1986

April. Interest-rate ceiling on bank loans of less than A$100,000 for owner-occupied housing approved after 3 April was removed. Interest-rate subsidy to assist savings banks to maintain their existing deposits.

June. Exposures to individual clients or groups of related clients in excess of 10 percent of shareholders' funds of the banking group to be reported regularly to the reserve bank.

July. Interest paid by offshore banking units (OBUs) on foreign currency deposits of nonresidents exempted from interest withholding tax. All lending by OBUs must be to nonresidents. Dividend withholding tax and branch profits tax abolished.

August. Maximum permitted foreign ownership of authorized dealers raised from 25 to 50 percent.

September. Banks established before 1981 required to maintain minimum capital ratios in the vicinity of 6 percent of total assets, 1 percent higher than previous minimum. Trading banks established after 1981 required to keep a minimum capital ratio of 6.5 percent.

November. Relaxation of restrictions on investments at interest in Australia by foreign governments and their agencies. Enactment of Cheques and Payment Orders Act providing for, inter alia, new checklike instruments (payment orders) to be drawn on certain nonbank financial intermediaries.

December. Savings banks allowed to deposit with or lend money to a parent or subsidiary savings bank.

1987

January. Prior notification to be given to the reserve bank of intention to enter into exceptionally large exposure to an individual client on the part of a banking group.

March. Restrictions on authorized money market dealers' holding of assets with more than five years to maturity removed.

April. Reserve-assets ratio applying to savings banks reduced from 15 to 13 percent. Ratio to be removed from savings banks regulations to become part of the prudential arrangements administered by the reserve bank. Deposit interest subsidy scheme for savings banks, introduced in April 1986, not renewed.

May. Government announced decision to amend the Banking Act of 1959 to make the reserve bank's powers over prudential supervision of banks more explicit.

October. Proposal to amend the Commonwealth Banks Act to enhance competitiveness of the Commonwealth Banking Group by enabling it to provide a wider range of services, including insurance.

1988

January. Reserve bank would trade with the public in small parcels of Treasury bonds.

August. Abolition of statutory reserve deposit requirement, which would be replaced by a new noncallable deposit set at 1 percent of both trading and savings bank assets. Treasurer announced the intention to abolish the distinction between trading and savings banks.

Appendix 2

Chronology of New Zealand Financial Deregulation[10]

1984

July. 20 percent devaluation of the New Zealand dollar. Removal of controls on lending and deposit rates, except on trading bank deposits of less than thirty days and ordinary 3 percent savings accounts. Marginal ratio policy applicable to finance companies removed.

August. Reserve bank discount window opened to all holders of government bonds with a maturity of less than six months. Abolition of the "thirty day rule," which had prevented payment of interest on trading bank deposits of less than thirty days. Removal of restriction that limited the rate of interest payable on ordinary savings account to 3 percent. Removal of the 1 percent per month credit growth guideline.

September. Withdrawal of three export credit assistance facilities administered by the reserve bank: the Short-Term Export Credit Facility, the Back-to-Back Facility for Long-Term Export Finance, and the Rediscount Facility for Developing Markets. Removal of reserve bank approval of, and last resort loan support for, the four dealing companies operating in the official short-term money market.

October. Removal of restrictions on maturity and interest rates of private overseas borrowings.

November. Removal of restrictions on the access of overseas-owned companies operating in New Zealand to domestic financial markets. Removal of restrictions on New Zealand financial institutions borrowing offshore (but specific currency exposure limits were not removed).

December. Removal of restrictions on New Zealand residents purchasing foreign exchange for investment purposes.

1985

January. Reserve bank to begin paying interest on trading bank settlement account balances at an initial rate of 5 percent. Tap system for issuing Treasury bills replaced by tender system.

February. Abolition of all compulsory ratios on financial institutions, including the trading banks' reserve-assets ratio, public-sector security ratios for a wide range of institutions, and the housing/farming investment ratios that applied specifically to life insurance companies and pension funds. The Post Office Savings Bank voluntary ratio still remained.

March. New Zealand dollar floated.

November. New bank policy allows institutions to call themselves banks provided they satisfy the following conditions:

- issued capital at A$30 million, with at least A$15 million paid up

- substantial business in deposit and lending functions

- a well spread shareholding, or firm internal controls to protect depositors from undue loan concentration or connected lending

- demonstrable banking expertise, plus willingness and capacity to make a positive contribution to the development of the finance sector

- good standing in the financial community

No artificial limit on the number of institutions able to qualify for bank status. No distinction between trading and savings banks. Legislation to be introduced to strengthen the reserve bank's supervisory powers, which will aim at stability of the system rather than guarantees to individual institutions or depositors.

December. Increase in the interest rates paid on settlement balances and more frequent adjustments to maintain approximate stable relationship with market rates.

1986

March to May. Liberalization of the New Zealand Stock Exchange.

July. Budget—continued import liberalization and review of industry plans.

1987

June. Budget—sale of government assets to pay off debt. The government will sell shares in a number of its businesses including New Zealand Steel, the Development Finance Corporation, Petrocorp, and Air New Zealand.

December. An increase in the goods and services tax to 12.5 percent not earlier than October 1, 1988. A four-year program of tariff reductions on goods not subject to industry plans, and a two-step reduction in duties on cars.

1988

December. Roger Douglas sacked.

1989

January. A December quarter price increase of 1.2 percent gave a new annual inflation rate of only 4.7 percent.

CONCLUSION

The case studies presented in this volume make it clear that there are quite a number of ways to carry out successful policy research. An important requirement for all policy research is that it be done openly. Initially, research results are often held narrowly within the bureaucracy, but as the economy develops, research becomes more sophisticated and the policy debate must spread beyond the bureaucracy if it is to be effective. The economy has to move away from a situation in which a narrow bureaucratic group drives and sanctions research, generally through the provision of finance, though in some cases also by controlling data and limiting the circulation of outputs.

Policy decisions become more complex, with greater opportunities for trade-offs among social groups. Intergenerational issues become important: How much should a country save and invest, at the cost of consumption, in order to make future generations more prosperous? Issues such as environmental concerns and population aging make medium-term outlooks essential.

Several types of institutions can carry out research into these policy issues, and in most of the East Asian countries there are enough well-trained professionals to staff a number of them.

Universities remain essential for the research process because of their teaching role and the synergy of teaching and research. Their importance is at the theoretical and technical end of research and in opening up subjects and issues not likely to be tackled otherwise. University staff in the region have performed this role remarkably well. The best example is the critique of policies of the Marcos regime, *An Analysis of the Philippine Economic Crisis,* by the School of Economics of the University of the Philippines in 1984. The use of university staff as consultants by other research organizations within a country, as well as their travel abroad to professional meetings and for further training, is also important.

At an early stage of development, bureaucracies need a "one-stop shop," such as the Korea Development Institute, to serve a variety of ministries and provide think tank support for central coordinating units such as prime ministers and planning departments. In the Asia-Pacific region several research institutes, assisted by academic institutions in industrial countries, have played this role at early stages of development. In Hong Kong and Singapore the universities were able to develop appropriate research arms.

As a country's economy becomes more complex, policies become increasingly important to growth. But constantly changing policies are a cause of great difficulties for public and private enterprises. Countries that permit major decisions about economic progress to be made on narrow political lines do not grow effectively. Major economic policy issues, such as the social content of fiscal and monetary policy, must have broad political cohesion and continuity behind them. Such cohesion and the lack thereof has been one of the major differences between rapidly growing East Asian countries and many Latin American countries. A country's principal political forum, generally its parliament, requires independent advice to build a national sense of economic purpose. At such a relatively sophisticated and complex level of development, research efforts extend to universities, think tanks, and within the bureaucracy as implementing ministries such as transport and agriculture establish research arms. Bureaucratic conflicts ensue. For this reason several industrial countries have established independent councils of economic advisers that report directly to the head of government or parliament on the major economic issues facing a country. Usually led and staffed by well-known, independent professionals, such organizations play a key role in public education and in establishing a national research and debate agenda for the economy. As political liberalization follows economic liberalization in the leading East Asian countries, they will need such an institution to avoid fragmenting their national growth outlook.

The diversification of research out of the public sector becomes essential as the economy grows and the political debate widens. Business groups require research inputs into business decision making. In some East Asian countries business-oriented research units are developing fairly rapidly, either as components of business organizations or as independent consultants. Other nonofficial inputs into research also have to be developed. External, nongovernment funding is needed for university staff. Businesses will have to create public foundations if they want to ensure that their interests will be properly explored and explained. This is happening in some countries, but the scale has to be enlarged to ensure effectiveness.

The importance and effectiveness of research changes over time in developing countries. Concern is initially focused on relatively simple major issues such as the principal bottlenecks in agricultural development or the conflict between import substitution and export orientation. The principal approach to social and physical infrastructural development may well be through the cost-benefit analysis of industrial projects and their ranking according to socioeconomic returns. Further along the development path the research issues become deeper and the subjects expand. Sectoral issues emerge: Is the education sector efficient and effective? How do returns to various levels of education compare? How should postgraduate studies be developed? What is the appropriate role for private industry in vocational training? How should vocational training be funded? As this approach is extended to all sectors, a great deal of attention must be devoted to the synthesis that informs a country about the content of fiscal policies on the revenue and expenditure side, how fiscal policies relate to monetary policies, and the effect these have on the balance of payments.

As policy issues become more complex, the contribution of research to effective policy formulation should increase. As options expand, so does the need to explore alternative policy possibilities. Research will only contribute positively, however, if it is objective, if it proceeds by testable, carefully defined hypotheses, and if it is handled in a scholarly manner. Ideological tracts, whether they proclaim the superiority of markets or planning, will not make a positive contribution to policy formulation.

Good research leads to good policies because it is directed toward the elaboration and quantification of alternatives. But good research can only be identified through an informed, high-level debate. The process of debate takes place at many levels: in seminars, academic journals, political speeches, and the media. Such a debate is also important in building the consensus required to initiate a sequence of appropriate policies that will build the stability needed by economic units to work effectively. Development experience suggests that policy swings, like inappropriate policies, are inimical to growth.

Government and the private sector must be convinced through experience that research is worth funding. At the same time funding should not be on an extravagant scale. Research always has to be somewhat ahead of policy requirements, but it can not be too far ahead of policy makers or it will be wasted. If it is not debated and used, it is useless. Ultimately a national research agenda, academic and bureaucratic research, research by vested interest groups, and a national research body are needed to ensure an appropriate level of research activity for a country's individual needs.

Policy Issues

Economic liberalization is a slow and difficult process. If it does not accelerate, growth will begin to slow in the East Asian countries. The industrial countries will not continue to give such tough competitors special treatment. More important, the near-industrializing countries will be treading on their heels, pushed by China, India, and other competitors. Economic liberalization breeds political liberalization, and political democracy will threaten the political unity that has been so important to past economic growth if steps are not taken to remedy the situation. If the East Asian countries wish to continue rapid growth, each will have to form a consensus about the economic growth it wishes to pursue. This will require the institutionalization of research for a wide-ranging policy debate. Discussions at the seminar that led to this publication linked particular policy issues with research requirements.

Macroeconomic policies. Sound macroeconomic policies are a prerequisite to successful trade and industry reforms. Experience suggests that even successful countries could greatly improve their policy framework. Sang-Mok Suh (Republic of Korea) argued that when the Republic of Korea embarked on an export strategy it emphasized exchange-rate policy. The government later concentrated on fiscal policy. Financial markets are yet to be liberalized. Mohamed Ariff (Malaysia) pointed out that although fiscal and exchange-rate policies in Malaysia are sound, the country is experiencing a flight of capital because the financial sector remains overregulated. Excessive regulation of the financial sector is a common limitation of macroeconomic policy.

Microeconomic policies. In the initial stages of economic development, microeconomic policies often target industries that are thought to have forward and backward linkage effects. It is doubtful if this is efficient, but it is certain that an interventionist approach of "picking the winners" becomes more and more inefficient as the economy expands and also creates increasingly serious international friction. In countries seeking rapid growth the focus then turns to market mechanisms and more neutral policies such as investment in infrastructure.

Effective microeconomic policies targeting productivity across industries require substantial information, as does the evaluation of benefits and costs in, for example, private direct foreign investment. Many countries do not have such data and research capacity.

Both Narongchai Akrasanee (Thailand) and Mari Pangestu (Indonesia) argued that appropriate macroeconomic policies, together with policies that concentrate on creating a competitive market environment, should take the place of sectoral policies.

Duck-Soo Han (Republic of Korea) pointed out the continuing importance of microeconomic research by noting that economy-wide policies, such as technology and manpower policies, have sectoral effects that are not necessarily neutral. Many microeconomic problems do not necessarily require detailed census data: sample surveys complemented by clear analysis can be extremely useful.

Chulla Azarcon (Philippines) argued that the Philippines would benefit from independent studies of the long-run effects of liberalization in different markets. Duck-Soo Han (Republic of Korea) added that the Republic of Korea would appreciate more information about the relative effects of industrial targeting and the effect of low uniform tariffs. Comparative studies of alternative development paths are important.

Sequencing of policy reforms. Economic theory suggests that slowly adjusting markets be liberalized first. Thus factor markets should be adjusted before product markets, which in turn should precede financial market liberalization. Macroeconomic policies should be liberalized before microeconomic policies in order to increase the effectiveness of the latter. In real life, however, political factors determine the implementation sequence, forcing countries to liberalize those sectors in which liberalization is politically feasible. Any policy-liberalization agenda needs to be continually reviewed and adjusted.

A logical political sequence for policies was proposed by Henry Ergas (Australia). Some policies constrain others. Financial liberalization constrains the government to fiscal prudence. Favorable early results from a particular liberalization may mobilize political support, constraining future policies and limiting opportunities for policy reversal. Suiwah Leung makes the same argument in her chapter on Australia and New Zealand.

Policy researchers must determine how to foster a political climate that favors liberalization. Academics, bureaucrats, and politicians must be convinced that liberalization is desirable. A vigorous open public debate should inform the media and the public. The role of an independent council of economic advisers is again essential.

Commitment, realism, and coordination. Indonesian experience demonstrates the success that can follow major "big bang" reform. Overnight replacement of all customs department officials by a private company successfully signaled a serious commitment to reform on the part of the Indonesian government. Signaling a commitment is vital if reforms are to be sustainable; without it, reforms are seen as negotiable, and vested interests mobilize to oppose them. Strategies for increasing the sustainability of reforms differ between countries. For some a successful strategy consists of a series of mutually supported deregulation moves; for others it can consist of broadly based reforms with effective implementation supports.

Chinese experience confirms the need for political realism. Successful rural reform in China between 1978 and 1984 conformed to traditional patterns of production at the same time it facilitated a response to market incentives. Urban reforms, by contrast, threatened the entrenched political power system and have been unsuccessful. Zhao Dadong described the implementation of reforms as involving "crossing the river by feeling the stones." China has plunged into a river that is deeper than expected and policy makers are having difficulties in reaching the stones. No special interest lobby has been organized to support economic liberalization.

Coordination of economic policies within the cabinet is an important factor of economic reform. Thus reform is difficult in the Philippines because vested interests are in conflict with reformers at the cabinet level. Indonesia, in contrast, has an effective Ministry of Economic Coordination because there is popular and high-level support for reform. Both process and structure are important in effective policy making.

In China economic reform has been characterized by a lack of coordination of reform measures. Combined with limited reform follow-up, reforms have had limited positive effects and have led to corruption.

The Role of Government

Political groups in East Asia have had both growth and equity objectives for the economy, and when in government they adopt policies that reflect these objectives. Malaysia's experience has shown government to be flexible in balancing growth and equity considerations: after a period of recession followed the highly equity-oriented New Economic Policy of the 1970s, there was a major return toward growth objectives in the 1980s.

In Indonesia trade and industry reforms since 1983 have also been both growth and equity oriented. The Indonesian experience indicated that a policy package should unfold without hesitation and thus create a momentum of reform. Sound macroeconomic policy is essential as a backdrop to reform, and policies and objectives have to be politically realistic. Clear and consistent objectives have to be linked with policy actions. Institutional mechanisms for communication between government and business have to be in place.

In conclusion, both the substance of policy (macro and micro) and policy making are important in managing economic liberalization. With respect to the latter, two broad issues were identified as important: the internal decision-making apparatus and the external independent policy-evaluation function. Further exploration of this internal-external paradigm, especially on an international comparative basis, would illuminate the role of research in economic liberalization.

NOTES AND REFERENCES

Chapter 1 has no notes or references.

Chapter 2   **Narongchai Akrasanee, "The Role of Policy Research in the Trade and Industry Reforms of Thailand"**

References

Bank of Thailand. *Monthly Bulletin,* various issues.

Income Statistics of Thailand. various issues.

Ingram, James C. 1971. *Economic Change in Thailand: 1850–1970.* Stanford: Stanford University Press.

Narongchai Akrasanee. 1980. *Industrial Development in Thailand,* Report of the Research and Planning Department, Industrial Finance Corporation of Thailand (in Thai).

Thailand Industrial Management Corporation. 1985. *Industrial Restructuring Study for the National Economic and Social Development Board.*

Chapter 3   **Mohamed Ariff, "Managing Trade and Industry Reforms in Malaysia"**

References

Ariff, Mohamed. 1975. "Protection for Manufactures in Peninsular Malaysia." *Hitotsubashi Journal of Economics,* 15, no. 2: 41–53.

Ariff, Mohamed, and Hal Hill. 1985. *Export-Oriented Industrialisation: The ASEAN Experience.* Sydney: Allen & Unwin.

Chan, Heng Wye. 1971. "Economic Planning in Malaysia." Graduation exercise, Faculty of Economics and Administration, University of Malaya, Kuala Lumpur.

Chee, Peng Lim. 1986. *Small Industry in Malaysia.* Kuala Lumpur: Berita Publishing Sdn. Bhd.

Fong, Chan Onn. 1985. "Structural Changes and Adjustments in Malaysian Industry." ASEAN-Australia Joint Research Project. Australian National University. Mimeo.

Jalil, Abdul. 1985. "Question Time in Malaysian Parliament." Graduation exercise, Faculty of Economics and Administration, University of Malaya, Kuala Lumpur.

Lee, Kiaong Hock. 1985. "Malaysian Manufacturing Protection Ideas, Structure, Causes and Effects." ASEAN-Australia Joint Research Project. Australian National University. Mimeo.

Muzaffar, Chandra. 1985. "The Decline of Parliament." *Aliran Monthly* 5, no. 4 (April/May): 1–4.

Naidu, Suranthiran. 1972. "The Intellectual Elite: Their Role in National Policy Making." Graduation exercise, Faculty of Economics and Administration, University of Malaya, Kuala Lumpur. Mimeo.

Power, J. H. 1971. "The Structure of Protection in West Malaysia." In *The Structure of Protection in Developing Countries*, ed. B. Balassa. Baltimore: The Johns Hopkins University.

Semudram, Muthi. 1985. "The Management of the Malaysian Ringgit." Institute of Strategic and International Studies, Kuala Lumpur.

Tan, T. N., 1973. "Import Substitution and Structure Change in the West Malaysian Manufacturing Sector 1959–1970." M.Ec. thesis, Faculty of Economics and Administration, University of Malaya, Kuala Lumpur.

Tilman, Robert. 1964. "Policy Formulation, Policy Execution and the Political Elite Structure of Contemporary Malaya." In *Malaysia, A Survey*, ed. Gungwu Wang. London: Frederick A. Praeger.

Verbruggen, Harmen. 1984. "The Spread Effects of Manufactured Export Production in Developing Countries." In *Export-Oriented Industrialization and Employment: Policies and Responses*, ed. Van Dijck and H. Verbruggen. Manila: Council for Asian Manpower Studies.

Wheelright, E. L. 1965. *Industrialization in Malaysia*. Cambridge: Cambridge University Press.

World Bank. 1955. *The Economic Development of Malaya*. Washington, D.C.

Yap, Kon Lim. 1972. "Role of the Foreign Advisers in Malaysia: A Study of the Cultural, Social, and Administrative Problems." Graduation exercise, Faculty of Economics and Administration, University of Malaya, Kuala Lumpur.

Chapter 4   In June Kim, "Evolution of Reforms and Structural Adjustment in the Korean Economy"

References

Cho, Yoon Je. 1988. "The Effect of Financial Liberalization on the Efficiency of Credit Allocation." *Journal of Development Economics* 29 no. 1: 101–10.

———. 1988. "Liberalization of Korea's Financial Market in the 1980s." Seoul. Mimeo.

Franco, de Silvio, Alberto Eguren, and David Baughman. 1988. *Korea's Experience with the Development of Trade and Industry*. EDI Policy Seminar Report no. 14, Washington, D.C.: World Bank.

Kim, In June. 1985. "Trade Policies of Korea." *The Seoul National University Economic Review*. (December).

Korea Development Institute. 1985. *Structural Adjustment and Industrial Policy Issues in Korea and Germany*. Seoul.

———. 1985. *Industrial Policies of the Republic of Korea and the Republic of China*. Seoul.

Republic of Korea, Economic Planning Board. 1988. *Economic Prospects and Policy Issues after the Olympics*. Seoul.

Republic of Korea, Government. 1988. *The Revised Sixth Five-Year Economic and Social Development Plan*. Seoul.

Republic of Korea, Presidential Commission on Economic Restructuring. 1988. *Report of Presidential Commission on Economic Restructuring*. Seoul.

Suh, Sang Mok. 1988. *The Evolution of the Korean Economy: A Historical Perspective*. Working Paper of the Korea Development Institute. Seoul.

Whang, In Joung. 1986. *Korea's Economic Management for Structural Adjustment in the 1980s*. Working Paper 8606 of the Korea Development Institute. Seoul.

———. 1988. "Role of Policy Research Institutes in National Economic Management: The Korean Case." Korea Development Institute, Seoul. Mimeo.

Young, Soogil. 1986. *Import Liberalization and Industrial Adjustment in Korea*. Working Paper 8613 of the Korea Development Institute. Seoul.

———. 1987. *Korea's Trade Policy Problems: A Comprehensive Review*. Working Paper 8720 of the Korea Development Institute. Seoul.

Chapter 5   Zhao Dadong, "Trade and Industry Reforms and Policy Research in China"

References

Bian Zhenghu and Li Gang. 1988. "On the Strategy of Grand International Circulation." *China: Development and Reform*, no. 6.

Cao Yuanzheng. 1988. "On Export-Oriented Economy." *Xinhua Digest*, no. 2.

Chen Yizi, Wang Xiaoqiang, et al. 1986. *Reform: Challenges and Choices*. China Economic Publishing House.

Cheng Xiaonong, Song Jinggong, et al. 1989. "Report on China's Economic Development of 1987." *Economic System Reform Studies Report, 1988–89*.

China Customs Administration. Various years. *Customs Statistical Yearbook*.

Diao Xinshen, Wang Xiaolu, et al. 1988. *Structural Contradictions in Industrial Growth*. Sichuan People Publishing House.

Dror, Yehezkel. 1984. "Required Breakthroughs in Think Tanks." *Policy Sciences*, no. 16.

ESRIC, Information Department. 1987. *Extraordinary Eight Years—A Chronicle of Development and Reform in China*. Sichuan People Publishing House.

Gao Shangguan, et al. 1988. *China: Development and Reform— 1987*. Sichuan People Publishing House.

Guo Fansheng and Wang Wei. 1988. *Poverty and Development*. Zheijiang People Publishing House.

Jing Liangjun. 1988. "Characteristics and Development of Foreign Think Tanks." *Decision Making Studies* 2, 3, 4, and 5.

Keesing, Donald B. 1979. *Trade Policy for Developing Countries*. World Bank.

Lu Cuanding. 1977. *International Trade*. Zhengzhong Publishing House.

Shi Pingsheng and Liu Ximin. 1988. "Growth of Newly Developed Industries and the Restructuring of Enterprises Organization." *China: Development and Reform*, no. 2.

State Planning Commission, Production Distribution Studies Office. 1989. "Come Out of the Double Pressure: China's Western Part Economy under the Coastal Developing Strategy." *China: Development and Reform*, no. 1.

State Statistical Bureau. Various years. *Statistical Yearbook of China*.

Sun Shangging, ed. 1984. *An Economic Structure Game Plan*. China Social Science Publishing House.

Xia Xiaolin. 1988. "Export-Oriented Economy and the Organizational Innovation of the Big and Medium Enterprises." *China: Development and Reform*, no. 12.

Zhao Yifang. 1988. "Ways to Further Perfect Contract-Responsibility System in Foreign Trade." *Foreign Trade Studies*, no. 41.

Zhou Bajun. 1988. "The Turning Point of the Reform and Opening Policy: The Economic Development Strategy of the Coastal Areas." *China: Development and Reform*, no. 6.

Zhou Qiren et al. 1987. *New Growth of National Economy and Rural Development*. Zhejiang People Publishing House.

Chapter 6   **Raul V. Fabella, "Trade and Industry Reforms in the Phillipines, 1980–1987: Performance, Process, and the Role of Policy Research"**

References

Alburo, F., R. Bautista, et al. 1986. *Economic Recovery and Long-Run Growth: Agenda for Reforms*. Manila: Philippine Institute of Development Studies.

Alburo, F., and D. Canlas, et al. 1985. "Towards Recovery and Sustainable Growth." University of the Philippines School of Economics. Unpublished monograph.

Alburo, F., and G. Shepherd. 1986. *Trade Liberalization Experience in the Philippines, 1960–84*. Philippine Institute of Development Studies Working Paper. Manila.

Baldwin, R. E. 1975. *Foreign Trade Regimes and Economic Development: The Philippines*. New York: Columbia University Press.

Bautista, R., and J. Power. 1979. *Industrial Promotion Policies in the Philippines*. Manila: Philippine Institute of Development Studies.

Becker, Gary S. 1983. "A theory of competition among pressure groups for political influence." *Quarterly Journal of Economics* 98: 371–400.

de Dios, E., D. Canlas, et al. 1986. *An Analysis of the Philippine Economic Crisis*. Quezon City: University of the Philippines Press.

Dingcong, C. 1987. "Foreign Borrowing, Debt-Servicing Capacity and Economic Growth: The Philippine Experience" M. A. thesis.

IBRD. 1987. *Report 6706-PH, The Philippines: Issues and Policies in the Industrial Sector*.

Medalla, E., and J. Power. 1986. *Trade Liberalization in the Philippines: Assessment of Progress and Agenda for Future Reform*. Tariff Commission–Philippine Institute of Development Studies Joint Research Project, Staff Paper 8691.

Montes, M. 1985. *Macroeconomic Adjustment in the Philippines: 1983–1985*. Philippine Institute of Development Studies Working Paper No. 87–01. Manila.

Montes, M. 1988. "The Business Sector and Development Policy." In *National Development Policies and the Business Sector in the Philippines*, ed. Ishii, de Jesus Edilberto, et al. Tokyo: Institute of Developing Economies.

National Economic Development Authority. 1987. *Medium-Term Philippine Economic Development: 1987–1997*. Manila: National Economic Development Authority.

Power, J., and G. Sicat. 1971. *The Philippines: Industrialization and Trade Policies*. London: Oxford University Press.

Sicat, G. 1974. *New Economic Directions in the Philippines*. Manila: National Economic Development Authority.

————. 1986. *A Historical and Current Perspective of Philippine Economic Problems*. Manila: Philippine Institute of Development Studies and the National Economic Development Authority.

Tecson, G. 1987. *Export Promotion Policy in the Philippines*. University of the Philippines School of Economics Working Paper.

United States Agency for International Development, Philippines. 1987.

Chapter 7   **Mari Pangestu, "Managing Economic Policy Reforms in Indonesia"**

References

Bhattacharya, A., and J. Linn. 1988. *Trade and Industrial Policies in the Developing Countries of East Asia*. World Bank Discussion Paper no. 27. Washington, D.C.

Indonesia. *State Budget, 1987–88*.

MacIntyre, Andrew. 1988. *Politics, Policy and Participation: Business-Government Relations in Indonesia*. Ph.D. diss., Australian National University.

Pangestu, Mari and Boediono. 1986. "'The Structure and Causes of Manufacturing Sector Protection in Indonesia." In *The Political Economy of Manufacturing Protection: Experience of ASEAN and Australia*, ed. Christopher Findlay and Ross Garnaut. Sydney: Allen and Unwin.

Pangestu, Mari, and Achmad Habir. 1989. "Trends and Prospects in Privatization and Deregulation in Indonesia." *ASEAN Economic Bulletin* (March).

Sastromihardjo, S. 1985. "Inpres No.4/1985: titikberat pada sasaran jangka pendek." *Prisma 7*.

Wardhana, Ali. 1989. "Structural Adjustment in Indonesia: Export and the 'High Cost' Economy." Keynote address at the Twenty-Fourth Conference of Southeast Asian Central Bank Governors, Bangkok, 25 January.

Woo, Wing-Thye. 1988. "The Economic Policy Making Equation in Indonesia." Paper presented at the Conference on Blending Economic and Political Analysis of International Relations, Claremont College, California, May.

Chapter 8   Suiwah Leung, "Financial Liberalization in Australia and New Zealand"

Notes

1. Statutory monetary powers in New Zealand date from the creation of the reserve bank in 1934. Instruments of monetary policy were not extensively used until the 1950s, and the range and scope of the controls available to the bank increased sharply in subsequent decades.

2. The offset coefficient is the coefficient of changes in net domestic assets. The latter is used as a right-hand-side variable in an equation explaining capital flows. Changes in net domestic assets are taken to be indicative of monetary policy, with a coefficient of minus one indicating that monetary policy is completely offset by capital flows.

3. The Reserve Bank of New Zealand confirmed that most of the net outflow appears to have arisen from the ability to alter the timing of the payment for imports and the repatriation of export receipts; however, the possibility of capital transactions being disguised as current transactions cannot be ruled out, particularly because some New Zealand merchant banks were also authorized foreign-exchange dealers at the time.

4. Note that nominal exchange rates for Australia and New Zealand are defined as units of foreign currency per unit of domestic currency. Hence, a rise in the nominal exchange rate means an appreciation of the domestic currency. Also, real exchange rate is defined, in the IMF fashion, as sP/P^*, where P refers to the domestic price level, s refers to the spot nominal effective exchange rate, and P^* refers to the composite price level of the country's trading partners. Effective exchange rate is identical to the trade-weighted exchange rate.

5. Inflation fell from 18.9 percent in mid-1987 to 5.6 percent in the year to September 1988. The 18.9 percent included a 10 percent value-added tax introduced on 1 October 1986. Nevertheless, the current New Zealand inflation rate is at or below that of its trading partners.

6. The wages pause and then the accord between the government and the Australian Council of Trade Unions came after a particularly difficult year of high inflation and unemployment in 1982–1983. The initial accord has undergone several changes, but the basic agreement consists of various trade-offs for direct nominal wage indexation to the consumer price index, including personal tax cuts and superannuation contributions from employers.

7. Official cash rate refers to the interest rate on overnight and call money in the official money market where the Reserve Bank of Australia deals with the official money market dealers in its market operations. In this context official does not mean administered.

8. In a more recent study, de Grauwe (1988) found some evidence to support the theory that overvaluation of real exchange rates leads to protectionist measures that are not removed during periods of undervaluation. Hence, exchange-rate variability reduces trade. Nevertheless, de Grauwe notes that declines in the growth rates of GDP in the OECD countries that he studied are, by far, the most important factor behind the reduction in trade growth among these countries. Yet regressing changes in trade on changes in GDP obviously entails simultaneity problems in the single equation model that he has estimated.

9. Harper 1986, 38; Reserve Bank of Australia *Bulletin*, May 1986, June 1987, and June 1988.

10. Reserve Bank of New Zealand 1986, 200–207; Bollard and Buckle 1987, 361–62; Reynolds, Chiao, and Robinson 1989.

References

Australia, Committee of Inquiry into the Australian Financial System. 1980. *Interim Report*. Canberra: Australian Government Publishing Service.

————. 1981. *Final Report*. Canberra: Australian Government Publishing Service.

Australia, Treasury. 1981. *The Australian Financial System*. Treasury Economic Paper no. 9. Canberra: Australian Government Publishing Service.

————. 1988. "Treasurer's Address to the Asia Society and American/Australian Association, New York, 4 October" and "Treasurer's Address to the British Australian Chamber of Commerce, London, 11 October." In *Treasury Press Release No.108*.

Australian Bankers' Association. 1979. *Submission to the Committee of Inquiry into the Australian Financial System*.

Australian Financial Review. 1988a. "And Now for a Breather." 13 October.

————. 1988b. "Lange Slows Privatisation." 13 October.

————. 1988c. "NZ Inflation Rate Falls but Union Unrest Mars Outlook." 17 October.

————. 1988d. "For Farmers, Rogernomics Is a Dirty Word." 17 October.

————. 1988e. "The Renovated Accord Prognosis: Beyond Resuscitation." 25 October.

Beetham, R. M. 1987. "The Government Strategy for the Economy and the Financial Industry in Australia." Address to the Australian Administrative Staff College, September.

Blundell-Wignall, A., and B. Thorp. 1987. *Money Demand, Own Interest Rates and Deregulation*. Research Discussion Paper 8703. Sydney: Reserve Bank of Australia.

Blyth, C. 1987. "The Economists' Perspective of Economic Liberalisation." In *Economic Liberalisation in New Zealand*, ed. A. Bollard and R. Buckle, 3–24. Wellington: Allen & Unwin.

Bollard, A., and R. Buckle. 1987. "Economic Liberalisation in New Zealand." In *Economic Liberalisation in New Zealand*, 361– 62. See Blyth 1987.

Buckle, R. A. 1987. "Sequencing and the Role of the Foreign Exchange Market." In *Economic Liberalisation in New Zealand*. 236–60. See Blyth 1987.

Carew, E. 1985. *Fast Money*. Sydney: Allen & Unwin.

Carey, D. A., and K. G. Duggan. 1986. "'The Abolition of Exchange Controls." In *Financial Policy Reform*, 153–66. Wellington: Reserve Bank of New Zealand.

Corden, W. M. 1988. *Australian Macroeconomic Policy Experience*. Invited Paper, Australian Economics Congress.

Deane, R. S. 1986. "Financial Sector Policy Reform." In *Financial Policy Reform*. Wellington: Reserve Bank of New Zealand.

de Grauwe, P. 1988. "Exchange Rate Variability and the Slowdown in Growth of International Trade." IMF Staff Papers 35, no. 1:63–84. Washington, D.C.

Dornbusch, R. 1976. "Expectations and Exchange Rate Dynamics." *Journal of Political Economy* 84: 1161–76.

Edwards, S. 1984. "The Order of Liberalization of the External Sector in Developing Countries." *Essays in International Finance* no. 156. Princeton.

Frenkel, J. A. 1983. "Panel Discussion on Southern Cone." IMF Staff Papers 30, no. 1: 164–73. Washington, D.C.

Harper, D. A., and G. Karacaoglu. 1987. "'Financial Policy Reform in New Zealand." In *Economic Liberalisation in New Zealand*. See Blyth 1987.

Harper, I. R. 1986. "Why Financial Deregulation?" *The Australian Economic Review*, no. 1: 37–49.

International Monetary Fund. 1984. *Exchange Rate Volatility and World Trade.* Occasional Paper 28. Washington, D.C.: IMF.

Kane, E. J. 1981. "Impact of Regulation on Economic Behavior." *The Journal of Finance* 36, no. 2: 355–66.

Keeler, T. E. 1984. "Theories of Regulation and Deregulation." *Public Choice* 44: 103–45.

Krueger, A. O. 1984. "Problems of Liberalization." In *World Economic Growth*, ed. A. C. Harberger. San Francisco: ICS Press.

Leung, E. S. 1988. "A Portfolio Balance Model of the Australian Dollar Exchange Rate." Draft Ph.D. diss., The Johns Hopkins University, Baltimore.

Mathieson, R. 1986. "'International Capital Flows, Capital Controls, and Financial Reforms." In *Financial Policy Reform in Pacific Basin Countries*, ed. Hang Shing Cheng. Lexington, Mass.: Lexington Books.

McKinnon, R. I. 1982. "'The Order of Economic Liberalization: Lessons from Chile and Argentina." *Proceedings, Carnegie-Rochester Conference Series on Public Policy* 17: 159–86.

Morgan Guaranty Australia Ltd. *World Financial Markets*, various issues.

Morris, D. 1988. "Monetary Transmission in a Deregulated Financial System." Paper presented at the Australian Economics Congress in Canberra, August.

Murray, G. L. 1978. "Monetary Policy and Capital Inflow." *Economic Record* 54: 271–80.

Obstfeld, M. 1983. "Exchange Rates, Inflation, and the Sterilization Problem." *European Economic Review* 21: 161–89.

Organization for Economic Cooperation and Development. 1987. *OECD Economic Outlook—Historical Tables*. Paris: OECD.

Polasek, M., and M. K. Lewis. 1985. "'Australia's Transition from Crawling Peg to Floating Exchange Rate." *Banca Nazionale del Lavoro Quarterly Review* (June): 187–203.

Porter, M. 1974. "The Interdependence of Monetary Policy and Capital Flows in Australia." *Economic Record* 50 (March): 1– 20.

Reserve Bank of Australia. 1979. *Submission to the Committee of Inquiry into the Australian Financial System*. Occasional Paper No. 7 of the Reserve Bank of Australia. Sydney.

———. 1984, 1985, 1986, and 1987. *Report and Financial Statements*. Sydney: Reserve Bank of Australia.

———. November 1985. "The Monetary System in Transition." R. C. Mills Memorial Lecture delivered by the Governor at the University of Sydney, October. *Bulletin*.

————. February 1986. "The Role of a Central Bank." Address by the Governor to the 39th International Banking Summer School at La Trobe University, Melbourne, February. *Bulletin*.

————. May 1986. *Bulletin*.

————. December 1986. "Open Market Operations since the Float." Paper presented by I. J. Macfarlene, Chief Manager, Financial Markets Group, Reserve Bank of Australia, to the Victorian Branch of the Economic Society, Melbourne, November. *Bulletin*.

————. June 1987. *Bulletin*.

————. September 1987. "Monetary Policy—The Lessons of History." Shann Memorial Lecture delivered by the Governor at the University of Western Australia. *Bulletin*.

————. October 1987. "Measures of Financing." *Bulletin*: 13– 21.

————. November 1987. "Banking—Post Deregulation: The Australian Experience." Cook Memorial Lecture of the New Zealand Bankers' Association delivered by the Governor in Wellington. *Bulletin*.

————. June 1987. *Bulletin*.

Reserve Bank of New Zealand. April 1985. *Reserve Bank Bulletin*.

————. August 1985. "A Review of Government Stock Tendering." *Reserve Bank Bulletin*.

————. 1986. *Financial Policy Reform*. Wellington.

Reynolds, R., Y. S. Chiao, and B. Robinson. 1989. "Macroeconomic Policies and Agricultural Sector Responses." Paper presented to the 33rd Annual Conference of the Australian Agricultural Economics Society, Christchurch, New Zealand, February.

Sanders, D. N. 1988. "Restructuring the Economy: Requirements and Prospects." Address given by D. N. Sanders, Managing Director, Commonwealth Bank of Australia, at a conference organized by the Asia Society and the American/Australian Association, New York, June.

Sinclair, K. 1980. *A History of New Zealand*. London: Allen Lane.

Spencer, G., and D. Carey. 1988. *Financial Policy Reform—The New Zealand Experience, 1984–1987*. Reserve Bank of New Zealand Discussion Paper G88/1 (April).

Stevens, G., S. Thorp, and J. Anderson. 1987. *The Australian Demand Function for Money: Another Look at Stability*. Reserve Bank of Australia Research Discussion Paper no. 8701. Sydney.

Swan, P. L., and I. R. Harper. 1982. "The Welfare Gains from Bank Deregulation." In part 1 of *Australian Financial Systems Inquiry, Commissioned Studies and Selected Papers*. Canberra: Australian Government Publishing Service.

van Wyngen, G. 1988. "Trans-Tasman Arbitrage Surprise." *Australian Business* (26 October).

Wells, G. 1987. "The Changing Focus of Fiscal Policy." In *Economic Liberalization in New Zealand*. See Blyth 1987.

PARTICIPANTS

Australia

Brian Brogan	Research associate, National Centre for Development Studies, Australian National University
Andrew Elek	First assistant secretary, Economic and Trade Development Division, Department of Foreign Affairs and Trade
Henry Ergas	Professor, Graduate School of Management, Monash University
Senator Gareth Evans	Minister of Foreign Affairs and Trade
Robert Gregory	Professor of economics, Research School of Pacific Studies, Australian National University
Darryn Gribble	First assistant secretary, North, East, and Southeast Asia Division, Department of Foreign Affairs and Trade
Tony Hely	First assistant secretary, Trade Strategy Branch, Department of Foreign Affairs and Trade
Chris Higgins	Deputy secretary, Coordination and Management Division, Treasury Department

Helen Hughes	Professor of economics and executive director, National Centre for Development Studies, Australian National University
Will Martin	Senior research fellow, National Centre for Development Studies, Australian National University
Peter McCawley	Deputy director general, Australian International Development Assistance Bureau
John Richardson	Director, Trade Strategy Branch, Department of Foreign Affairs and Trade
Ilze Svenne	Assistant secretary, Asia Branch, Department of Foreign Affairs and Trade

China

Yang Jian Hua	Associate research fellow, Department of Policy Research and System Reform, Ministry of Foreign Economic Relations and Trade
Zhang Gui Xiang	Deputy director, Department of Policy Research and System Reform, Ministry of Foreign Economic Relations and Trade
Zhao Ren Wei	Director, Institute of Economics, Chinese Academy of Social Sciences

Economic Development Institute of The World Bank

Hyung Ki Kim	Advisor, Institutional Development
Vinyu Vichit-Vadakau	Senior training officer, National Economic Management Division
Russell Cheetham	Director, Asia Regional Office

Indonesia

| Billy Joedono | Assistant to minister, Department of Industry |

Republic of Korea

Duck-Soo Han — Director general, Bureau of Small and Medium Industries, Ministry of Commerce and Industry

Sang-Mok Suh — Member of the National Assembly and deputy chairman of the Policy Committee of the Democratic Justice Party

Malaysia

Abdul Ghani Othman — Deputy minister of Energy, Telecommunications, and Post

Abdullah bin Mohamed Tahir — Head, Industry Division, Economic Planning Unit, Prime Minister's Department

Papua New Guinea

Samson Polume — Economist, Department of the Prime Minister

Philippines

Chulla Azarcon — Chairwoman, Tariff Commission

Senator Vicente Paterno — Chairman, Economic Affairs, Philippine Senate

Thailand

Chakramon Pasookvanich — Director, Government–Private Sector Cooperation, National Economic and Social Development Board

Narongchai Akrasanee — Executive vice president, Thailand Development Research Institute, member of Policy Advisory Council of the Prime Minister

Prachuab Chaiyasan — Minister of Science, Technology, and Energy

for not explicitly promising EU membership. This criticism reflects the slow progress in the region and the inability of the EU to act effectively and be the strong and decisive partner in this very unequal and asymmetric partnership.[15] At times, however, far too much is expected from the EU in the pursuit of a very wide agenda. This is because we tend to forget that the EU is not a nation-builder, hardly a state-builder, nor can all governmental policies be designed exclusively from outside. The EU type of state-building regards the state primarily as an agency that should deal with the implementation of the *acquis communautaire*, rather than as the interaction of the state with its citizens. This is a static and more technical understanding of the state which assumes that once efficiency is attained a country is automatically democratic and legitimate. In addition, the EU is not a development agency; at times the criticism is even levelled that its policies and demands go against the developmental needs of the poor economies of the Balkans. The EU is not a panacea for all local problems although it can suggest solutions, impose templates and conditions and offer resources to back them up.

CONCLUSION

The variety of challenges the EU faces in the Western Balkans is overwhelming as far as the europeanisation and European integration of those countries is concerned. It will take a number of years before the backward and inexperienced Western Balkan countries are ready for membership. To meet those challenges, the EU has to have a sense of purpose and vision for the future. The fourth Copenhagen criteria on the readiness of the EU to accept more members is often neglected. So far it has been taken for granted that the EU can accommodate more members and that its enlargement instrument can have benevolent repercussions for both the EU and the candidate countries. Yet, the digestion of eastern enlargement and the prospect of Turkish membership have already generated turmoil inside the EU. Even Romania's membership, notwithstanding some notable successes at the political, ethnic and economic levels, raises doubts as to whether the EU is lowering its standards in its effort to accommodate more enlargements. European publics and their leaders are rather confused as to what is the meaning and the benefits of the enlargement process. In many ways, the biggest challenge is within the EU itself; solving its own existential question will help address all of the difficult Balkan questions.

[15] Anastasakis, O. 'The Europeanization of the Balkans' *The Brown Journal of World Affairs*, 12 (1) 2005, pp. 77–88.

CONTRIBUTORS

MOHAMED ARIFF has worked in the Faculty of Economics and Administration of the University of Malaya and is currently a professor of analytical economics. Professor Ariff has published extensively in the areas of industrial development and international trade and has been involved in ASEAN economic cooperation programs.

RAUL V. FABELLA is associate professor at the University of the Philippines School of Economics where he teaches microeconomic theory, trade theory, and mathematical economics. His current research interest is in applied trade and industry policy. He has published in cooperative team theory and has forthcoming publications in rent-seeking theory and risk in rural households.

IN JUNE KIM is currently associate professor at the Department of International Economics of Seoul National University. From 1985 to 1986 he was deputy director of the Institute of Economic Research, Seoul National University and concurrently appointed a member of the advisory committee of the Ministry of Finance. He also served as a consultant to the Economic and Social Commission for Asia and the Pacific in Bangkok and the United Nations Educational Scientific and Cultural Organization in Paris. Dr. Kim has specialized in international economics, international finance, and macroeconomics.

SUIWAH LEUNG is a visiting fellow to teach at the National Centre for Development Studies, the Australian National University. She has had work experience at the Reserve Bank of Australia, at the Australian Taxation Review Committee, the Office of National Assessments, and at the Centre for Resource and Environmental Studies, Australian National University. She has published papers on exchange markets, electricity demand, Indonesia's economic outlook, ASEAN, income tax, and minimum income guarantees.

NARONGCHAI AKRASANEE is executive vice president of the Thailand Development Research Institute. He is also a member of the Policy Advisory Council to the prime minister of Thailand and an industrial policy adviser to the National Economic and Social Development Board.

SYLVIA OSTRY held teaching and research positions at a number of Canadian universities and the University of Oxford Institute of Statistics. In 1964 she joined the Canadian federal government where she held the posts of chief statistician, deputy minister of consumer and corporate affairs, chairman of the Economic Council of Canada, deputy minister of international trade, ambassador for multilateral trade negotiations, and the prime minister's personal representative for the economic summit. From 1979 to 1983 she was Head of the Economics and Statistics Department of the OECD in Paris. Her most recent publications include *International Economic Policy Coordination* (with Michael Artis); *Interdependence: Vulnerability and Opportunity*; "Regional Trading Blocs: Pragmatic or Problematic Policy?" (with Michael Aho); *The Global Economy: America's Role in the Decade Ahead*.

MARI PANGESTU is a research associate at the Centre for Strategic and International Studies and concurrently teaches at the Faculty of Economics, University of Indonesia. Her area of specialization is international trade policy.

ZHAO DADONG was appointed to the Economic System Reform Institute of China as senior research fellow and head of the Department of International Cooperation in 1988. He specializes in the area of government participation in macroeconomic controls.

INDEX

175

ICEG Academic Advisory Board